"There are so many ways for kids to travel this path, and Kelly Storck offers a road map that makes the journey joyful. With compassion and humor, *The Gender Identity Workbook for Kids* lets little ones lead the way."

—**Brook Pessin-Whedbee**, author of *Who Are You?*

"*The Gender Identity Workbook for Kids* is the first of its kind to offer immediate support for kids exploring their gender. Written in a clear and concise manner, this book takes young readers on a journey of information and celebration about their authentic selves."

—**Johanna Olson-Kennedy, MD**, specialist in the care of gender-diverse children, adolescents, and young adults; and medical director of the Center for Transyouth Health and Development at Children's Hospital Los Angeles

"Kelly Storck's *The Gender Identity Workbook for Kids* is comprehensive—if you've thought about it, you'll likely find it in this book. Concepts are explained clearly, and with sensitivity, insight, caring, and compassion. Storck offers sage advice and support—it feels as if she is right there with you. This book is a valuable resource to go back to frequently on the gender journey of self-discovery, deeply affirming of the uniqueness and worth of every person."

—**Stephen M. Rosenthal, MD**, professor of pediatrics at the University of California, San Francisco (UCSF); cofounder and medical director of the UCSF Child and Adolescent Gender Center; immediate past president of the Pediatric Endocrine Society; and vice president of the Endocrine Society

"DeShanna: I really enjoyed the different activities this workbook had to offer for both parents and kids. I also believe this is a workbook that could help medical and mental health providers, as well as educators, understand more about the gender spectrum of the young gender-diverse people they work with. This workbook can change the narrative and change hearts and minds.

Trinity: I really liked all of this book; however, my favorite part was seeing all the trans people throughout history that have helped us progress. I really loved that many of them looked like me, a black trans girl, and gave me more hope and confidence that I too can make history and the world an even better place."

—**DeShanna Neal**, public advocate and mother of **Trinity Neal** (public advocate and transgender girl)

"Comprehensive and relatable, this workbook is a much-needed, invaluable tool for gender-expansive kids and those who are seeking to understand them! Kelly is the perfect person to write such a book, and she brings her signature compassion, empowerment, support, and strength to every page. The first of its kind for younger gender-expansive kids, this workbook will help them understand and communicate their uniquely personal experience of gender. Here's to the opening of hearts and important conversations!"

—**Darlene Tando, LCSW**, has a private practice in San Diego, CA; has been working with gender-expansive and transgender youth/adults since 2006; and is author of the book *The Conscious Parent's Guide to Gender Identity*

"*The Gender Identity Workbook for Kids* is just what it says it is: instant help for parents and kids. We have needed a gender guide for kids, families, and providers, and Kelly Storck has created the perfect companion. The book includes fun, simple language, great graphics, and useful activities to navigate school, families, friends, and the inner journey to understand and then rejoice in one's own gender. Thank you, Kelly!"

—**Jen Hastings, MD**, director of the Transgender Healthcare Program, Planned Parenthood Mar Monte; Medical Advisory Board, UCSF Center of Excellence for Transgender Health; director of Medical Programming, Gender Spectrum

"This is the book that I've been waiting for! Many parents with a gender-expansive child worry early on that they may 'push the child to be transgender' by allowing them to express their gender differences. And many well-meaning adults worry that other parents, therapists, and medical professionals will also push a child towards transitioning. This book answers each of those concerns. By providing a young person with bite-sized lessons about both identity and expression, and asking thought-provoking, open-ended questions, kids are offered a chance to figure out exactly who they are and where they fit on their own, with no pressure and no judgement. It's past time for us to have such a valuable tool, and I'm excited about being able to suggest it and share it with parents, teachers, and anyone who regularly works with youth."

—**Debi Jackson**, parent of a transgender daughter, trans youth advocate, speaker, and trainer

"*The Gender Identity Workbook for Kids* is something I wish I'd had when our daughter transitioned, but so thankful to have now! We found the activities relevant, eye-opening, and age-appropriate for both of our children. Most importantly, it got us talking as a family about topics that we may not have discussed, and opened up conversation about being inclusive of others in ways we hadn't yet tackled. In addition, I've spent my entire career as an educator, and have seen schools slowly integrating conversation and activities around gender identity into many programs. This book will be a true game changer in that space, allowing schools to use portions where needed, or, as a unit to address school social-emotional goals. We often forget that that all people have a gender identity, and this workbook truly makes that evident, ensuring that regardless of a child's identity, we are all unique, special, and worthy of celebrating!"

—**Vanessa Ford, MAT**, parent advocate

"The Gender Identity Workbook for Kids is a gift to families whose young children may be struggling to come to terms with and realize unique identities. Kelly's comprehensive work has the potential to transform a potentially anxiety-ridden time into one of celebration and fruition. This is the first guide I have seen that skillfully and compassionately guides children, living in today's social environments, to handle difficult questions and attitudes they might face from peers. *The Gender Identity Workbook for Kids* is a much-needed contribution to the library of any parent or caregiver of a gender-nonconforming child. I certainly wish this book had been available when we began our journey with our transgender son. Brava!"

>—**Mimi Lemay**, author, and member of the Human Rights Campaign's
>Parents for Transgender Equality Council

"The Gender Identity Workbook for Kids is a *must-have* for parents, gender-diverse kids, and professionals who work with them. Kelly Storck has put together a phenomenal set of activities that increase understanding of gender-diverse people's history and bodies, and teach the much-needed real-world skills of how to answer other people's questions about your gender. I am thrilled to have this in my clinical toolbox to recommend to families for years to come."

>—**Colt Keo-Meier, PhD**, child/family clinical psychologist, expert in
>gender health private practice, and University of Houston psychology
>department lecturer

"Kelly's amazing workbook offers children and adults of any gender the opportunity to learn and explore who they are and why. Using prompts, activities, and inclusive illustrations, Kelly is able to create a safe and affirming context for self-discovery and understanding the spectrum of gender. If I had access to a book like this when I was young, it would have changed my life and helped the adults who love me see my authentic gender much earlier. Thank you, Kelly, for putting out this invaluable tool and resource that guides us in talking about gender with kids! It is a conversation all of us should be having!"

>—**Mere Abrams, MSW**, writer, educator, researcher, and gender specialist
>in the San Francisco Bay Area

"The Gender Identity Workbook for Kids creates a world where we can explore what's inside of us, what makes us feel most like ourselves. Kelly Storck has created a place of possibility, where anyone can choose to take up the deep and delightful journey of exploring their gender(s). This book is an invaluable resource that no doubt teaches each of us that read it something new about ourselves."

> —**Alic Custer-Shook**, pediatric emergency nurse, and doctoral student at the University of Washington who mentors transgender youth, and is a speaker on gender diversity

"The Gender Identity Workbook for Kids is a fun and accessible tool all kids can use to explore gender and identity. Kelly Storck does an awesome job at turning the complicated questions about gender diversity into tangible and helpful 'takeaways' for everyone in the family. I am sure kids, parents—and anyone interested in creating a more inclusive world—will love this workbook!"

> —**Jean Malpas, LMHC, LMFT**, founder and director of the Gender & Family Project at the Ackerman Institute for the Family, director of international training, and psychotherapist in private practice in New York, NY

The Gender Identity Workbook for Kids

A Guide to Exploring Who You Are

KELLY STORCK, LCSW

Instant Help Books
An Imprint of New Harbinger Publications, Inc.

Publisher's Note

Distributed in Canada by Raincoast Books

Copyright © 2018 by Kelly Storck
Instant Help Books
An imprint of New Harbinger Publications, Inc.
5674 Shattuck Avenue
Oakland, CA 94609
www.newharbinger.com

Cover design by Amy Shoup

Acquired by Wendy Millstein

Edited by Ken Knabb

Illustrated by Noah Gringi

Library of Congress Cataloging-in-Publication Data on file

20   19   18

10   9   8   7   6   5   4   3   2   1   First Printing

Littles, I am a profoundly better person because of you.

Contents

Section 2: Understanding Me

Section 3: Being Me

Acknowledgments

This *Gender Identity Workbook for Kids*, at least as written by me, would never have existed without Diane Ehrensaft. When she told me, "I won't stop until you publish," I thought her kind but misguided. She believed not only that I *could* write this book, but that I was exactly the person who *should* write this book. Eventually, I believed her. Thank you, Diane, for your faith and support all along the way.

This book is penned from my heart, at least as much from my mind. I am honored to walk through life amid many amazing gender-diverse people. The enlightened spirit and brilliant love I find in their souls is an absolute gift. I write with them in my heart and am so grateful for the light they bring into the world.

I am also lucky to work among some amazing people—gender-diverse people, parents of gender-diverse children, and gender specialists—who inspire and challenge me. The work is long and hard, but we are fierce and determined. Love and truth always win, and I am proud to be a part of the revolution.

Noah Grigni—you are an artistic genius with a big heart and an amazing lens. I am so grateful to have done this with you. Thank you for bringing the pages alive.

Alic, my gratitude for you radiates out in many directions. You are a dear friend, a wise soul, a powerful voice, and a magnificent possibility model.

Finally, I can hardly put into words the immense pride and joy I experience being a parent. Raising my children is indisputably the most important and gratifying work of my life. Sonshine and Moo—thanks for being exactly who you are. I love you forever. No matter what. And to my partner through it all: I thank you not only for the pretty stuff but especially for all the good, hard work it takes to make it possible.

Foreword

I have two very warm memories—one is strolling down the streets of Amsterdam with Kelly Storck and a group of our colleagues, all of us gender specialists, and just feeling Kelly's warmth, excitement, and insight. She stopped to insist we all take a group photo, which I will always cherish. And the other—sitting with a broad smile as Kelly hit it out of the park at a Gender Spectrum conference with a stupendous talk that gave us professionals in the audience a detailed road map for helping children transition from one gender to another. They say that good things always come in threes—so now we have the third, Kelly Storck's *The Gender Identity Workbook for Kids*, which you are now going to have the great pleasure of diving into.

Very recently I was asked to speak to a group of child psychiatrists who wanted to learn more about all the kids who either say they are not the gender everyone thinks they are or don't want to do gender the way everyone says they should—our transgender and gender-diverse little people. One of the members of the group, who I know well, stopped me afterward and asked, "I have a seven-year-old person I'm working with who is very upset about the body they have because it doesn't match the gender they know themselves to be—do you have anything I could recommend for them to read?" "Why yes," I said, "I have just the book for you. As a matter of fact, it's right here in my bag—*The Gender Identity Workbook for Kids: A Guide to Exploring Who You Are*. Try 'Activity 8—All Kinds of Bodies,' or 'Activity 16—My Body.'" That couldn't have happened even a year earlier. Why? Because all the authors seemed to be forgetting about the kids in the middle—the ones who weren't very little but weren't grown up yet. The ones who were in grade school and had all kinds of questions about their gender and all kinds of things they wanted help with or wanted to learn. They were too old for all the little kid picture books, and there was no way they were going to make sense of those small-print books with no pictures that all the older kids were reading. And why should everyone forget about them, particularly when they were showing up to be the fastest growing, biggest group of people who have come forward to say, "Hey, look at me. I'm part of the new gender revolution, just by being me"? That "me" might be a transgender young person, or a person who says "I'm a boy/girl, I'm both," or "I'm a gender Prius—a hybrid," or "I'm a gender Smoothie, a gender blender." Whoever you might be, you deserve the attention that all the littler and bigger people are getting, and now you have it with the *Gender Identity Workbook for Kids*.

The first time I met them, Meredith (not their real name because we want to protect their privacy) looked at me earnestly and announced, "I know who I am, but I don't know how to do it." Translated: "Everyone thinks I'm a girl, but I know I'm a boy. But how do I let people know and how do I make that happen?" Meredith isn't the only one asking that question. It's not easy having everyone assume you're the gender that is a perfect match for the "Male" or "Female" stamped on your birth certificate, when you know that doesn't feel right. It's not any easier feeling like you don't fit into either gender box—girl or boy—but that you're something in the middle or something outside gender boxes altogether. Or maybe you're someone who is gender ambidextrous—you can use your girl self as easily as your boy self and you can switch off any time you want, if only people will let you. Or maybe you're just a boy who likes to wear dresses—if only people won't laugh at you. It's nice to have a road map to "know how to do it." Kids need one, parents need one, actually everyone needs one because these are new, unmarked trails for a lot of people.

We live in a world where gender seems to be very important. Why else do we always ask, "Is it a boy or a girl?" before the baby is even a person and it's still growing inside the mother? All that is to say that we live our genders every day, from our smallest activities to our wildest dreams. If you're a gender-creative, gender-expansive, gender-diverse kid, that can prove to be a big challenge, because a lot of people don't understand about the gender you are or the way you want to "do" it. As Kelly Storck tells us, "We all need to have some help to keep us feeling safe, loved, and valued when times get hard." And that's what she's going to do for you in this workbook—get into the nitty-gritty of figuring out how to be your very truest gender self, even when the going gets tough. She's going to take us where the rubber hits the road—like what do you tell other kids about who you are? What bathroom should you use? What happens when you don't like the body you have, because it's not a good match for the gender you are? In the workbook Kelly Storck reminds all of us that "you, your gender, and your needs are so important." That means we all have to figure out how to make sure that your gender gets all the attention it deserves and that those needs are met. So here is some good news. The book you're holding in your hands right now is going to make that happen. So go for it!

—Diane Ehrensaft, PhD

Hello, Parents!

Welcome! Whether you come to this book with eagerness or hesitancy, joy or sorrow, fear or peace, I am glad you found your way here. My hope for this book is that children who experience gender differently feel affirmed and understood. These kids come with adults who love them and you, as one of those adults, are likely feeling overwhelmed or unsure or worried as you do the work of raising and supporting a gender-diverse child.

I hope *The Gender Identity Workbook for Kids* offers light by providing information about gender in ways that reflect the experiences of your gender-diverse child. I hope this book gives your child both a mirror so they can see themself with greater clarity and a microphone so they can use their voices to help you and others understand what they need. When things come into better focus, I hope this book serves as a guide with lots of possibilities, all aimed at supporting the happiest and healthiest life for your growing child.

Throughout the process of uncovering your child's gender experience, it is crucial that your child know you love, trust, and respect them enough to follow their lead. The best way to use this book is to let your child take that lead. You may find it helpful to ask your child if they'd like to work through the book on their own or if they'd rather you sit and talk them through the book. If they want to start on their own, assure them you will be nearby if or when they need you.

I imagine you may have many questions, so I have created an online supplement that addresses common questions and includes helpful resources. You can find it at www.newharbinger.com/40309 (see the very back of this book for more details). I hope you and your child find what you need here. Wishing you all the comfort, insight, and love you need to walk this journey together.

Hello, Kid!

I am so glad you have this book. This workbook is about what can happen when you feel or express your gender in ways that are different from what people expect. This workbook has three sections—"Understanding Gender," "Understanding Me," and "Being Me"—that will help you learn more about gender, more about your unique gender, and how to be the happiest, healthiest, truest version of yourself. As you work through the pages here, I hope you will find ways to understand and love yourself and your unique and individual gender. I also hope you find your way to the things you need to help you live your happiest and healthiest life.

This book is designed so you can simply start from the first activity and follow along in order. However, you may want to skip through things that don't seem to fit you or that are too hard to work on right now, and that's okay. Most of this book is made just for you, but there are parts that encourage you to share with a helpful adult. Start thinking about who you might like to invite along with you as you explore this book and the feelings that come up for you as you work through it.

I am super excited you are here, and I, for one, already know you are an amazing person. I hope lots of other folks show you how wonderful you are, but in case you are scared or unsure, please know that you are important. This book is here to help you!

Section 1

Understanding Gender

This section helps you understand more about gender. Gender can be challenging to wrap your head around because many of us don't have all the information about what gender really is (or isn't), or we have information that isn't completely correct. To makes things more clear and helpful, I've gathered some lessons here that will help you understand the ins and outs of gender and get to know your unique gender better.

What Is Gender?

For You to Know

Understanding gender can be complicated, but knowing your own gender might be rather simple.

When babies are born, one of the first things people want to know is, "Is it a girl?" or "Is it a boy?" It's like people need to know the answer to these questions before they know how to think or feel about another person. Some people think if they know the *sex* of a person, they know the *gender* of a person. They believe these two words mean the same thing. Nope. No. Wrongo!

The label of "boy" or "girl" given to a baby at birth and a person's gender are two different things, and for some people the two are quite different. This might sound complicated, but knowing your own gender can be rather simple. Most importantly, each person has the right to know and declare their own gender. You are the expert when it comes to your gender!

Understanding something complex takes time, and it's helpful to break big ideas into smaller ideas. So let's break gender down into smaller parts…

Assigned sex is a label of "boy" or "girl" based on a look between a newborn baby's legs. This is the label of male or female that goes on a baby's birth certificate. People have a mistaken belief that having a penis means you are a boy and having a vulva means you are a girl. (You will learn more about bodies in Activity 8.) The truth is that bodies come in many forms and lots of children do not fit this mold.

Gender expression is the way people "wear" their gender. We express gender in lots of ways, including the way we style our hair, the clothes we wear, what we like to do, and how we act. Our world has lots of expectations about how girls and boys are supposed to look and act, and these gender "rules" can feel pretty uncomfortable if you like to express yourself differently.

Gender is your deep-down feeling that you're a boy, a girl, neither, both, or something else. That's right! Not just a boy OR girl—some people know themselves to be BOTH boy and girl or NEITHER boy nor girl or SOMETHING ELSE altogether. There are so many genders, and the expert on your gender is YOU!

For You to Do

These are really important ideas, so let's check that we are on the same page.

1. How do people assign a baby's sex?

2. What do we call the way a person *expresses* their gender?

3. Who is the absolute best person to know and declare your gender?

Answers:

1. By looking at the baby's body. Remember, this assigned sex is not always the same as a person's gender!

2. Gender expression.

3. YOU!!!

Apples and Oranges Activity 2

> ## *For You to Know*
>
> There are many different ways to experience and understand gender. It is important for people to understand your gender the way you know it so that you feel affirmed and supported.

When we try to compare two things that are so different that comparing them isn't useful, we say "it's like comparing apples to oranges." A wise therapist friend of mine, Dr. Diane Ehrensaft, uses this "apples to oranges" idea to showcase the importance of knowing the differences between two groups of children. As she describes it, the "oranges" are gender-expansive kids—kids who *express like* or who *wish to be like* another gender. The "apples" are transgender kids—kids who *are* another gender. It helps to know what description fits your experience of gender the best. This is important because all children need to be affirmed—recognized and celebrated for who they are—but many transgender kids need more than just affirmation in order to be their happiest, healthiest selves. Let's explore this some more…

Gender-expansive children have gender expressions that are different from what is expected of their assigned sex. Most gender-expansive children don't affirm a different gender identity. Since they identify with the gender associated with their assigned sex, these kids usually don't need changes to the labels and words people use for them—like girl/boy and she/he—and are less likely to grow up to be transgender adults. Examples of gender-expansive kids include boys who feel like boys *and* like to wear dresses, play princess, or wear their hair long. Or girls who feel like girls *and* like to play rough, love sports, refuse to wear a skirt, or like their hair short. There are all kinds of ways to be a boy or girl; some girls like "boy things" and some boys like "girl things." Sneak peek: Activity 10 talks about how these things, like toys and hobbies, don't care what gender a person has and explains that all kids should be able to like things without such a fuss about gender!

Transgender children have an assigned sex and gender that are different. These kids can look and act a lot like gender-expansive kids, but they don't just *act* or *look* like another gender, they *are* another gender. Examples include a child who was labeled a girl but who knows himself as a boy, or a child who was labeled a boy but who knows herself as a girl.

There are also children who have a gender other than male (boy) or female (girl). These are **non-binary children**. A "binary" is something made up of two parts—the way people often think of gender. But gender isn't actually made up of two parts, male or female; it can be any number of parts. Some non-binary kids feel like a blend of both a girl and a boy at the same time. Other non-binary kids feel their gender differently depending on where they are. For example, a person can feel like a boy at school and like a girl at home. Non-binary kids can also feel their gender move fluidly over time. A person can feel more like a girl one day or week and more like a boy the next day or week. They may be a mix of girl *and* boy, or identify completely separately from the boy-girl options. Examples include people who are *gender-fluid* (both boy and girl), *agender* (neither boy nor girl), or *genderqueer* (gender other than boy or girl).

Group	Labels	Gender expression	Gender identity	What do they need?
Gender-expansive	Girl Boy Tomboy Princess boy Pink boy Rainbow	Gender expression is outside what is expected for the child's assigned sex.	Gender identity is the same as assigned sex.	Affirmation: to be accepted for who they are. Often they simply need more room and support to express themself freely.
Transgender	Transgender boy Transgender girl Girl Boy	Gender expression is likely outside what is expected for the child's assigned sex.	Gender identity is different than assigned sex, yet still in the binary (boy or girl).	Affirmation (see above) plus... Alignment: Need for better fit with their gender may involve some form of transition.
Transgender, Non-binary	Gender-fluid Genderqueer Agender Bigender Third gender Demiboy/girl	Gender expression comes in a wide range, often with a mix of what's expected for boys and girls. Gender expression can be different on various days or in various settings (home or school).	Gender identity is different than assigned sex and is not found in the binary. Not strictly boy or girl, but a mix of boy and girl or a gender that lies beyond boy or girl.	Affirmation and alignment (see above) plus... Advocacy: They often need more support to create room for their non-binary identity to be seen and respected.

For You to Do

Take a look at the descriptions in the chart. On most days, do you feel more like a gender-expansive kid, a transgender kid, or a non-binary kid?

_____

What makes you feel like a gender-expansive kid, a transgender kid, or a non-binary kid?

_____

_____

_____

How does it feel to be a part of this group?

_____

_____

_____

Breaking Out of the Binary

For You to Know

Not everyone feels like a girl or a boy. Some people feel like neither, both, or something else altogether.

People often talk about gender as a binary—something made up of two parts—because they only see options for girls and boys. But this leaves out all the lovely people who have a gender other than boy *or* girl. Like people who are a boy *and* a girl. Or people who are *neither* a boy *nor* a girl. Or people who have different ways of experiencing and describing their gender that don't even use the idea of boy or girl. We can think of all these genders as "non-binary" because they are outside of the expected "boy" and "girl" boxes.

There are many ways to experience and describe a gender. The important thing is that knowing and being in your true gender, whatever you call it, helps you feel whole and right in the world. Feeling whole and right about ourself is something we all need. But this gets harder for people with genders outside of girl or boy. Many people don't understand gender beyond boy and girl, and this means that non-binary people often get left out. Feeling forced to choose between girl and boy all the time because there are no other options offered can be really stressful. And getting people to see and understand their gender or use their pronouns can be tiring. If you feel this way, it's even more important that you and the people close to you understand and affirm your unique gender so you can feel confident out in the world.

Let me introduce you to some kids who have genders that are outside of the boy and girl boxes. These kids have worked to understand and love themselves, their gender identities, and their gender expressions, even when that has proven hard.

Jaquise: Jaquise grew up with everyone calling them a girl. They knew this didn't feel right, but they also didn't feel like a boy. This was really confusing until Jaquise figured out that people don't have to identify as a girl or a boy or with any gender at all. Jaquise uses the word "agender" to describe their feeling of being outside of the gender spectrum—not having a gender, or having a gender that is neither girl nor boy.

Alex: Alex is a proud and creative person. Alex doesn't feel all boy or all girl. Alex can feel different parts of their gender in different settings, at different times, or all at once. Sometimes Alex is a boy, other times Alex is a girl, and sometimes Alex is both mixed together. People often want Alex to stick to one gender, which can make it hard for them. But Alex knows that just doesn't work. So they continue calling themself "gender-fluid" or "genderqueer"— which is how Alex describes the way their gender is a mix of girl and boy— even though it can be hard when people don't understand or accept Alex's experience.

Micah: Micah absolutely loves all things bright, sparkly, fancy, and fabulous. Micah mostly feels like a boy and he "loves all things girly!" People used to tease Micah because he was different, but Micah's friends and family helped show him that everyone, including Micah, should be able to do what makes them happy and comfortable. Micah is a gender-expansive kid who sometimes calls himself a Princess Boy, and he looks pretty awesome in his favorite dress!

For You to Do

These questions are designed for kids who have a gender outside of the binary. Feel free to skip this section if that description doesn't fit you.

In what ways do you feel like...

neither a girl nor a boy? _____

_____

both a boy and a girl? _____

_____

some other gender? _____

_____

If you have a gender that feels outside of just boy or just girl, what is it like to live in a world that appears to have only two options (boy/girl)?

_____

_____

If you could meet any of the kids described above, what would you like to ask them or tell them?

_____

_____

More to Do

All of the kids described in this activity have had some confusing or sad times related to their gender.

Share a time you felt teased, rejected, or hurt because someone didn't understand you or your gender identity.

_____

_____

_____

List three things that help you when you are feeling hurt or sad—things you can use to help make you feel happier and safer whenever you find yourself feeling down.

_____

_____

_____

Gender in the Animal World

For You to Know

Nature shows us that gender is naturally diverse and fluid.

Like us humans, many animals have a body and a gender that appear to fit neatly into male and female boxes. But many other animals, again like us humans, have amazing variations in bodies and gender. Let's explore some of these awesome creatures in the animal kingdom!

Fish: Many fish are born with body parts that are both typically male and typically female. These fish live part of their lives with the bodies and behaviors typical of one sex, then change and live with the bodies and behaviors of another sex. A few special fish can even change gender as many as ten times in their life span! These changes help the whole species thrive and grow.

Seahorses: Unlike most animals, the male seahorses become pregnant and give birth to baby seahorses. This is also true for humans. Having babies isn't just for moms—transgender dads sometimes give birth to babies also!

Frogs and Lizards: Many frogs and lizards start life out as one sex and then go through big changes as they continue growing. They might change their bodies and change the way they express their genders. A few lizards even change sex before they are born!

Butterflies: Some butterflies have two different wings—one that shows the animal as a girl and another that shows the animal as a boy. Non-binary butterflies!

For You to Do

What animal(s) described here sound most like you? _____

How are you like this animal? _____

_____

How are you different? _____

_____

Gender Around the World

For You to Know

Differences in gender exist all around our big, wide world.

You are learning that gender is expansive and that gender identities are limitless. Here are just a few examples of gender diversity around the world...

Hijra people in India

The Hijra people were assigned a sex of male at birth, and then they adopt a female gender role and most consider themselves as a third gender. Historically, Hijras were seen as powerful people who could grant great luck and were often sought after for blessings. There are at least half a million Hijra people in India and they have been present for thousands of years.

Hijras (India)

Two-Spirit people in North America

Many Native American belief systems hold that all living things have feminine and masculine qualities. In turn, many Native American tribes identify people who have both a feminine and a masculine spirit. These two-spirit people, as they are often called, assert themselves to be a mixed gender or a third gender. These people are often highly respected in their tribes and many great visionaries, dreamers, and shamans were two-spirit people.

Two Spirit (North America)

Māhū (Hawaii)

Māhū people in Hawaii and North America

Māhū people have a gender that is between male and female, or a mix of male and female. The Māhūs were highly regarded in Hawaii for a long time and often held positions as beloved healers, teachers, and caretakers. Māhūs were also given the important task of passing on traditions and Hawaiian wisdom. Want to know more? You can check out the PBS film *Kumu Hina*, about a transgender Hawaiian teacher and a young person proud to be a mix of male and female.

Bissu
(Indonesia)

Bugis people in Indonesia

The Bugis people (an island society in Indonesia) have five genders that exist in harmony. Aside from male and female, there are *Calabai* (men who take on female roles) and *Calalai* (women who take on male roles). The fifth gender, *Bissu*, is known as a "transcendent gender," and encompasses all genders or none at all. The Bissu hold important and sacred roles in their society.

Fa'afafine people in Samoa

Born with an assigned sex of male, Fa'afafine people have a strong female gender identity. Their parents often recognize this early on and let these children grow up more freely, generally raising them as girls or a third gender.

Fa'afafine
(Samoa)

For You to Do

1. In what ways do you feel like, or different from, any of the people described here?

     _____

     _____

2. If you could meet any of the people from the groups described above, who would you choose and what would you like to ask them or tell them?

     _____

     _____

More to Do

If you know any people who do gender differently, write about them here.

_____

_____

_____

_____

_____

_____

Gender Through History

People have been living outside the gender binary for thousands of years! It is important to look back so we can see that gender has always existed in many different ways.

Joan of Arc (1412–1431): I was a brave and wise French soldier in the Hundred Years' War. I refused to wear the clothes and hairstyles expected of women during a time when people could be punished or even killed for not following the "rules." People demanded that I act and look like they expected of a woman or face punishment, but I held firm to my right to express myself freely. My life was cut short when I was captured, tried, and executed for being a freethinker and nonconformist. Long after my death, I was declared a saint and am considered a national heroine for my brave leadership in the French military. I hope my story reminds the world how terribly unjust it is to punish people for being different.

Lucy Hicks Anderson (1886–1954): When I was born, everyone thought I was a boy, but I always knew that I was a girl. Being transgender was nearly unheard of back then, yet my mom took me to a doctor who told her it was okay to raise me as the girl I knew myself to be. Later in my life, some people accused me of lying and questioned whether I could really be a girl. I told them, "I defy any doctor in the world to prove that I am not a woman. I have lived, dressed, and acted just what I am, a woman." I lost a lot of rights because people thought I was trying to trick them by living my life as a transgender woman. I hope my story helps you gain the strength and wisdom to stand up for yourself when people don't understand what is means to be transgender.

Billy Tipton (1914–1989): I was a famous jazz musician who was assigned a sex of female and lived most of my adult life as the man I knew myself to be. Although I had a successful career and a loving family, I never told the people I loved most about having an assigned sex of female for fear they wouldn't understand. Feeling like I couldn't share my whole self with the people closest to me was often hard and sad. Thankfully, you are living in a time where more people can live free and open lives.

Sylvia Rivera and **Marsha P. Johnson** (1951–2002 and 1945–1992): Together we fought to help people who were poor and homeless. We were passionate about letting people be who they were and neither of us cared much for all the labels and judgments people would place on us. Together we started S.T.A.R., a shelter for transgender youth, and we worked hard to make a safer and fairer world for kids that were having a hard time, especially people of color who were gay or gender-diverse. We hope you will help continue this work of making the world a safer place for people!

MISS MAJOR
GRIFFIN - GRACY
1940 - PRESENT

Miss Major Griffin-Gracy (1940–present): I grew up in a time when few people understood what it meant to be transgender and I have had to fight my way through many difficulties. I have survived being kicked out of my family home, being homeless, fighting for trans rights in the 1969 Stonewall riots, and serving time in prison. I have devoted my life to advocating for justice and freedom, especially for trans women of color in the prison system. I am honored to be a respected transgender elder. Many people simply call me "Mama."

For You to Do

1. How are you like the people shown here? How are you different?

   _____

   _____

2. Which of these people would you most like to be able to talk with now? What would you ask them or tell them?

   _____

   _____

3. Many of these people helped make the world a better place for people of all genders. What do you want to share or do to help change the world?

   _____

   _____

4. If you could be in a book like this in 100 years, what would you like to have written about you?

   _____

   _____

   _____

   _____

We Are All Stars

For You to Know

Knowing you are an important part of a larger group of people can help make you feel safe, understood, and supported.

Gender is like a big universe full of different and amazing ways to be human. And if gender is a universe, we are *all* stars! Knowing people (or stars!) who look, feel, or think like you helps you know you are okay just as you are. It's important to have all kinds of different people in our life—family, friends, teachers, neighbors, and more. When we feel that we are a part of a bigger group, we call this "community." Without community, we can feel alone and left out. This can be especially true when you feel or look different than the people around you. If you don't have friends like you already, let me introduce you to a few stars from the gender universe!

Frankie (age 5) loves to play with his friends who are mostly girls, and he has worn something pink (his favorite color!) every day this year. Frankie is a boy who prefers many things that girls usually like. Sometimes Frankie refers to himself as a "girly boy," but he doesn't like it when people who don't know him call him that.

DeShaunna (age 8) loves to dance and sing. When she was young, people thought she was a boy, but DeShaunna always felt like something was "different." DeShaunna talked about her feelings with her parents, who came to know that she is a girl even though they had thought she was a boy. Now she gets to live her life in her true gender as a girl.

Almas (age 9) is an amazing artist who loves to draw characters and write stories. Almas doesn't feel like a boy or a girl. Almas uses they/them pronouns and instead of being seen as a girl or a boy, they prefer to be seen most simply as "me." Almas has a great group of friends who understand them.

Shen (age 11) loves sports and is proud of his new short haircut. People used to describe Shen as a tomboy—a girl who liked "boy things." That was fine for a while, but then Shen became uncomfortable being labeled as a girl, especially when his body started to change. People began to realize that Shen is not a tomboy—Shen is a boy. He was able to get on puberty blockers (you will learn more about puberty blockers in Activity 34) so his body felt more comfortable to him.

For You to Do

Looking back at the friends you just met...

1. Whose story is most like yours? _____

2. How are you the same? How are you different?

    _____

    _____

3. What parts of the stories did you find most exciting? Sad? Confusing?

    _____

    _____

    _____

4. My favorite story is _____ because _____

    _____

More to Do

It's your turn now! Write a bit about yourself and your experience of gender here:

_____

_____

_____

_____

_____

_____

All Kinds of Bodies

For You to Know

Bodies come in many wonderful forms, sizes, and colors. All
bodies are important.

Bodies are very important. Bodies help us breathe and play and learn—in fact, we
can't exist without them! Finding comfort in your body is important for your health.
So, what if you feel you have a "different" body or something doesn't feel quite right
about the body you have?

First, you should know that there are all kinds of bodies and each one of them is
important. In the past, people were taught that there are only two kinds of bodies—a
"boy body" and a "girl body." People believed that the parts of a person's body called
genitalia (usually covered by underwear) made a person's gender. Old lessons said
girls have vulvas (the vulva includes all the parts between the legs, including the
vagina, which you can't see on the outside) and boys have penises. But we are getting
to know better, right? Gender is something people know on the inside, not something
that can be known by looking at a person's body. There are many kinds of bodies and
many ways to know your gender identity.

It is true that many girls have vulvas and many boys have penises. It is also true that
some girls have penises and some boys have vulvas. And people with non-binary
genders (neither, both, or something else) have important bodies too. Plus, many
babies are born with bodies that don't fit the expectations of a "girl body" or a "boy
body"—kids who are *intersex*—and their bodies are just as important.

The Gender Identity Workbook for Kids

It's also essential to know that your body belongs to *you*. Bodies are extensions of us as human beings, and this means *you* are the expert when it comes to your body. You get to have any feelings and thoughts about your body and no one can be more right than you. If you feel uncomfortable using the words "penis" or "vulva" to describe your genitalia, you can use a different word that feels better for you. Some people aren't used to talking about bodies, but it will help to find someone who listens to you and respects your rights as the "owner" of your body.

Take a look at these examples of different bodies and gender expressions:

ALL BODIES ARE IMPORTANT

For You to Do

1. Find the body or bodies in the illustration that fit you best.

2. Using the pictures to help you, describe your unique combination of body, gender expressions, and gender identity.

    _____

    _____

    _____

3. What do you think about having this body and gender combination?

    _____

    _____

    _____

4. What do you like about your body?

    _____

    _____

    _____

5. What do you wish was different about your body?

    _____

    _____

    _____

More to Do

Remember that we all need our bodies to stay healthy. Even when there are parts of your body that don't feel right for you, it is important to do your best to keep your whole body safe and healthy.

1. Do you have parts of your body that are harder for you to like or to take care of because they don't feel right for you? If yes, which ones?

   _____

   _____

2. What feels hard about liking or taking care of those parts?

   _____

   _____

3. Name anything that does or could make it easier for you to like or take care of these parts of your body.

   _____

   _____

4. Name three things you already do to keep your body safe and healthy (like brush your teeth, go to the doctor for check-ups, eat healthy foods).

   _____

   _____

   _____

Pronoun Town

> ## *For You to Know*
>
> Only you can know what words are right to describe you, and it's important that you find the ones that fit for you.

What are pronouns? Pronouns are another way to acknowledge someone when you aren't using their name. They are small but powerful words that change according to a person's gender. Pronoun use can be difficult when people don't know or understand another person's gender and use incorrect words when referring to them. This can make a person feel uncomfortable and hurt. Perhaps you feel this way and are here for help.

Here is a quick table that shows the most common ways people use pronouns in the English language. In other languages, the options are different and may not include any gender-neutral pronouns, or all pronouns may be gender-neutral.

Pronoun	Usually used by...
She/Her/Hers	Girls
He/Him/His	Boys
They/Them/Theirs **Ze/Zir/Zirs**	Non-binary people—people who feel like both a girl and a boy, neither a boy nor a girl, or something else. They/them/theirs are also used when we don't know or do not want to assume a person's gender. For example, "Someone forgot their backpack."

The Gender Identity Workbook for Kids

Everyone in Pronoun Town gets to pick the pronouns that work best for them—that's super awesome! Let's get to know some of the people around town. Keep an eye out, maybe you will meet someone like you...

Nicki: Everyone around town used to think that Nicki was a boy, but Nicki has felt like a girl for a long time and just didn't know how to tell anyone. Being seen as a boy and getting he/him/his pronouns made Nicki anxious and uncomfortable. Last year, Nicki told a trusted adult about wanting to use she/her/hers pronouns. Nicki loves the way it feels, and now she and her family are happier.

Benji: Benji sometimes feels like a boy and sometimes feels like a girl. Most of the time, Benji doesn't feel like either a girl or a boy. Benji feels best when people use they/them/their pronouns for them. As folks in Pronoun Town were told about Benji's pronouns, they were happy to use the right words. This means Benji feels more comfortable and they can get back to the business of being a kid! A win for everyone!

Devonne: Sometimes people see Devonne as a boy. This feels pretty good until Devonne's parents "correct" people because they see Devonne as their daughter. Devonne shares that he/him/his pronouns usually feel best, but he would like some time to think about what pronouns feel right at home, at school, and with friends. Working through these thoughts and changes as a family helps Devonne feel supported and loved.

As you can see, changing pronouns might seem like a little change and sometimes it takes time for folks to figure it out, but it sure can make a BIG difference!

For You to Do

1. Circle the pronouns people use for you now. There is a blank space for you to add different pronouns if your pronouns are not on this list.

    He/Him/His   She/Her/Hers   They/Them/Theirs   Zi/Zir/Zirs   _____

2. How do you feel when people use those pronouns for you? Use feelings words like "happy," "sad," "mad," or "embarrassed," and do your best to describe why you feel this way.

    _____

    _____

    _____

3. The pronouns I feel fit me best are _____ because

    _____.

More to Do

Changing pronouns doesn't have to be an all-or-nothing thing—you can take your time to let it unfold as you are ready.

Do you want these people to use different pronouns for you? Answer with Yes, No, or Maybe, and add details as needed.

Immediate family (parents, siblings)? _____

_____

_____

Extended family (grandparents, cousins)? _____

_____

_____

School staff? _____

_____

_____

Friends? _____

_____

_____

Getting Gender Off Our Stuff!

For You to Know

Many people put things into one of two boxes—"for boys" or "for girls." But these things—like toys and clothes—don't care if you're a boy, a girl, both, neither, or something else.

OLD "RULES":

FOR BOYS   FOR ANYONE   FOR GIRLS

FOOTBALL
CARS
SHORT HAIR
BLUE
MATH
JOHN

GREEN
READING
PANTS
MUSIC

DOLLS
DRESSES
LONG HAIR
CHEERLEADING
PINK
JANE

In our world, we place a gender on nearly EVERYTHING. Toys, clothes, names, hair, activities, and colors all get shoved into boxes that say "This Is for Boys" or "This Is for Girls." The idea that things need to be separated is made up—meaning that instead of being real or occurring naturally, people created the "rule" and insist it is important to follow even though it doesn't really matter. This limits us all without good reason.

It's important for you to know that things don't come with rules—toys, clothes, names, hair, activities, and colors are for everyone. So how do you choose what is right for you? Forget the rules and let your heart lead you to the things that make you most happy and comfortable. These will be your things because they are right for you!

For You to Do

Do you have things you like that others say you shouldn't like? What are they?

_____

_____

How does it feel when people say you shouldn't like those things?

_____

_____

If you felt free to like anything you wanted to, what would you do differently with…

Toys? _____

_____

_____

Clothes? _____

_____

_____

Your name? _____

_____

_____

Hair? _____

_____

_____

Activities? _____

_____

_____

Colors? _____

_____

_____

For You to Know

You are growing all the time. Having supportive people in your life helps you grow up strong, healthy, and happy.

People are talking about gender a lot these days. This means that folks are getting smarter about how to make the world a better place for people of all genders. This knowledge is growing quickly, so we have to pay close attention. We now understand that children can know their gender at a young age and that children thrive when they are supported within their asserted gender. That makes sense because we all do better when we have a circle of helpers that love, respect, and celebrate us. With the help of some trusted adults, you can find ways to be a strong, healthy, and happy YOU.

Your commitments might include:

- Staying in touch with your feelings, thoughts, and needs;

- Finding trusted adults (parents, family, therapist, school staff) who care for you in ways that feel good and safe; and

- Sharing your thoughts, feelings, and needs with your trusted adults.

Your trusted adults' commitments might include:

- Being a good listener;

- Following your lead as the expert on your gender;

- Making sure you know you are loved just as you are; and

- Finding helpful resources that support everyone in the process.

Can you think of any adults who can do the jobs described above? If you have a hard time thinking of someone at first, consider looking for adults in your school, in your extended family (like an grandparent or cousin), or in activities you enjoy (coach or club leader). If you don't have anyone now or you don't want to share this activity, that's okay. Take some time to build connections to adults you can trust, so you will have someone to share with soon.

For You to Do

Let's practice this important work of learning and sharing. Invite a trusted adult to join you for this activity.

Adult: You have been chosen as someone this child trusts. Write a note here thanking them for choosing you and let them know what it means to you to fill this important role.

_____

_____

_____

Child:

1. Share a few thoughts about why you chose this person as a trusted adult.

    _____

    _____

2. How do you feel about sharing with this trusted adult?

    Worries? _____

    _____

    Hopes? _____

    _____

3. Share three things you want this trusted adult to know about gender or your gender identity.

    _____

    _____

    _____

4. What parts of gender or your gender identity do you want help understanding? Be open, because your answer will help this trusted adult find the information or support you need!

    _____

    _____

    _____

Adult:

1. Let the child know you heard them by reflecting back what they shared with you. You can tell them, but make sure to write it down here, too.

    _____

    _____

    _____

    _____

2. What promises do you make to this child as you provide them with support, information, and love?

_____

_____

_____

3. Share two ways this child can let you know if they want to talk.

_____

_____

Section 2

Understanding Me

Hopefully you are feeling more gender-wise after Section 1, because now it's time to apply that wisdom to your own experiences of gender. Section 2 offers chances to explore different parts of your gender identity and gender expression so that you can know (and love!) yourself with greater pride and confidence.

Finding Your Own Style

For You to Know

Choosing the clothes and hairstyles you like the best are great ways to express yourself.

Like everyone else, you get up and put on clothes as a part of getting ready for the day. You might like fancy clothes or sporty clothes or lots of different kinds of clothes. Clothes can be an easy way to show people how you feel and what you like, and clothes don't care if you are a boy, a girl, neither, both, or something else.

The same goes for the way you wear your hair. You can wear long hair or short hair, spiky hair or curly hair, hair up or hair down. You can even add some color or accessories to make your hair say, "This is me!"

The trouble is that lots of people separate clothes and hairstyles into the same boxes they sort things like toys: "This Is for Boys" and "This Is for Girls." This means that some people don't feel able to wear the clothes or hairstyles they like best. This is not fair. When it comes to clothes and hairstyles, whatever feels right for you is…RIGHT! And another great thing: If you like lots of different styles of clothes and hair, you can change it up as you go! Welcome to a place where you are free to love any or all the options!

Now that we have that cleared up, let's explore your unique style! You get to pick out all the clothes and hairstyles you like best. You can mix styles and colors to fit all the wonderful parts of you. There's even room for you to draw yourself in your favorite style!

Shop Around for Your Favorite Clothes.

For You to Do

1. What do you like about the clothes you picked?

    _____

    _____

    _____

2. How did it feel to be able to choose any kind of clothes for yourself?

    _____

    _____

    _____

3. If these clothes are different from what you wear now, how would it feel for you to wear these clothes at home? At school? Out on the weekends?

    _____

    _____

    _____

4. Make a real-life shopping list—what kinds of clothes would you like to have? Who can help you get these clothes?

    _____

    _____

    _____

Find the Hairstyles(s) You Like Best for You.

5. How does it feel to wear the hairstyle you have now?

    _____

    _____

6. How would you most like to wear your hair?

    _____

    _____

7. What do you think it would be like to change your hair? Who could help you change it?

    _____

    _____

    _____

    _____

The Gender Identity Workbook for Kids

More to Do

Design two of your favorite looks here. Mix and match your clothes and hairstyles to make looks that fit you best!

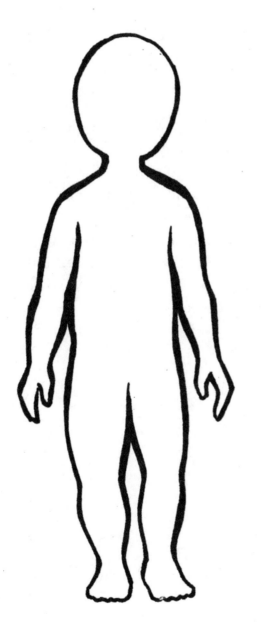 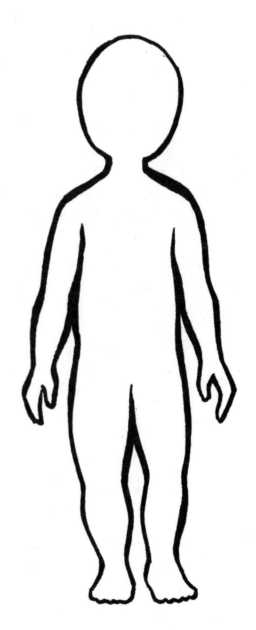

Toys Are Toys

For You to Know

All toys are for *all* kids (and adults too!). Play with whatever makes you happy!

Toys are made to help kids imagine, learn, and have fun. There are oodles of different kinds of toys like cars, dolls, blocks, balls, games, and many more wonderfully interesting things. What if you could play with every kind of toy EVER made? That would be awesome, right? Playing with different toys helps us figure out what we like, how we feel, and what brings us joy. Have you ever met a toy that refused to play with you because of your gender? NO, that's silly! Toys don't care if you are a girl, a boy, neither, both, or something else. So play with as many wonderful things as you'd like. And if someone says "That's for girls" or "That's for boys," you can let them know that "Toys are toys, and toys are for everyone!"

The Gender Identity Workbook for Kids

For You to Do

Mark some of the toys you like best from the illustration above.

What toys do you like to play with that people might be surprised you like?

_____

_____

Are there any toys or games you are afraid to play with because people might not understand why you like them?

_____

_____

Have you ever been teased about the toys you're playing with, or told you can't play with a certain toy or game?

Yes   No

If yes, what did that feel like for you?

_____

_____

_____

_____

Names Are Names

For You to Know

Finding a name that helps you feel proud to be yourself is important.

One of the first things we ever get is a name. The names we get follow us around wherever we go, and this makes them a very important part of our life. The thing is, we don't get to pick our names when we are born. Since many names suggest that a person is a boy or girl, sometimes parents end up picking a name that doesn't fit quite right. If your name doesn't feel right, it could be time to start thinking about names that can help you feel most like yourself.

For You to Do

How does the name given to you at birth feel or fit for you?

_____

_____

What nicknames or other names do you like for yourself? Circle the ones that feel the best.

_____

_____

_____

_____

What nicknames do not fit for you?

_____

Who uses the names and nicknames that fit best for you?

_____

_____

How does it feel when people use your chosen or preferred name or nickname?

_____

_____

More to Do

If you want to change your name, would you like to do that...

Now? Sometime later? Just at home?

_____

_____

Share any worries you have as we think about names.

_____

_____

_____

_____

My Body

For You to Know

Sometimes people can feel uncomfortable with their bodies. Understanding what you need from your body can help you feel happier and healthier.

Bodies come in different shapes and sizes, with different abilities and parts. There are all kinds of bodies, and each one of them is important; there's no body that's "wrong" or "not okay." But the fact that we have all these combinations means that sometimes people have a body that doesn't feel right *for them*. In fact, many people have something about their body that they wish they could change. This feeling can be especially strong for people who are transgender. Some transgender people have parts of their body they wish would go away. Other transgender people wish for different parts to appear or grow on their bodies. These needs for a different body can cause a lot of discomfort and sadness.

If you have these uncomfortable feelings about your body, it's important for you to understand what makes you feel this way. Knowing this can help you share your feelings with people who can help you find ways to make things more comfortable between you and your body. This might mean talking about your feelings or getting a hug or hearing that you are loved. And this might mean talking to doctors (see Activity 34) who can help you change your body so you feel safer and more comfortable. In the meantime, it's really important that you keep yourself and your body safe and healthy. If you ever feeling like hurting yourself or any part of your body, you need to find a trusted adult to talk to so they can help you.

For You to Do

Fill in these bodies with details like body parts and hair.

Body I Have Now

Body I Want

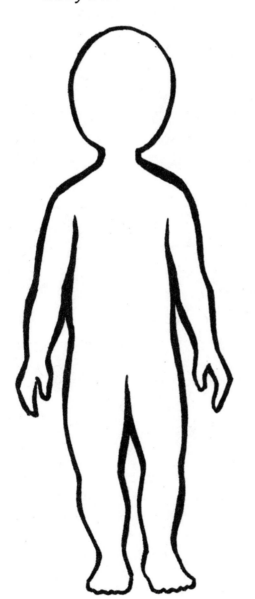

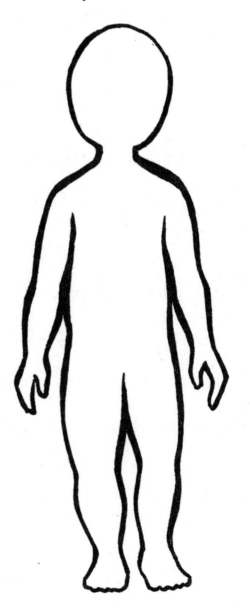

How does the body you have now feel to you? Use the scale here and write about your answer in the space provided below the scale.

0   10
_____

Don't like my body at all   Love everything about my body

_____

_____

What do you love about your body as it is now?

_____

_____

What do you wish was different about your body?

_____

_____

How do you feel when you imagine having the body you want?

_____

_____

The Gender Identity Workbook for Kids

More to Do

What parts of your body are harder to like or to take care of?

_____

_____

Do you ever think about hurting yourself or any part of your body?   Yes   No

If yes, be sure to share this with an adult so they can help. What thoughts do you have about hurting yourself?

_____

_____

_____

Circle two ways you can get some relief when you are having these uncomfortable thoughts and feelings.

Talk to an adult   Visit a doctor   Talk with a therapist

Play with a friend   Listen to music   Write about your feelings

Go to a support group   Read this book   Take deep breaths

Activity 16 We Can't Always See What's on the Inside

For You to Know

Sometimes it is hard to get others to understand and see our genders the way we want them to be seen.

Our gender is held deep inside us, and sometimes it isn't seen clearly by other people. People assume another person's gender identity most often by a person's body and gender expressions, like their hair, clothes, or name. For transgender and gender-expansive people, the way gender looks on the outside can be pretty different from the way it feels on the inside. Keeping parts of your gender identity or gender expressions inside where it can be private or just for you sometimes feels good. Other times, people keep their gender identity or expressions tucked away or out of view because they are worried they will be rejected or treated unkindly. This can feel very frustrating, scary, and sad because it means the gender-diverse person doesn't feel safe enough to be open about who they are, and then other people can't clearly see or reflect who the person knows themself to be. So if people don't seem to get your gender or how you like to express yourself, I am sorry for all the ways that is hard. There is good news here, though. The way you know your gender on the inside is the most true and important, and with some help you can figure out how to live in and express your gender so you feel seen and celebrated.

The Gender Identity Workbook for Kids

For You to Do

Draw and write whatever helps you show…

**What people see
on the OUTSIDE.**

**What I feel, know,
and like on the INSIDE.**

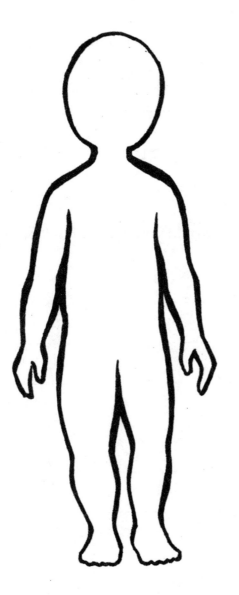
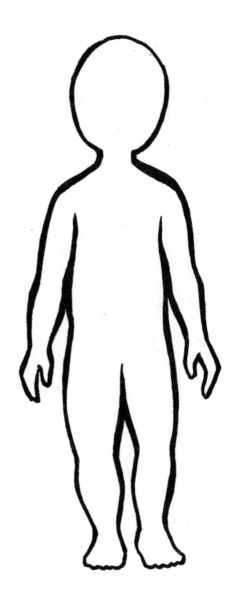

Activity 16 We Can't Always See What's on the Inside

What looks different about your gender or gender expression in the two pictures?

_____

_____

_____

What parts of your gender identity or gender expressions do you like to keep inside or private so it's just for you?

_____

_____

_____

What parts of your gender or gender expressions would you like to show more on the outside?

_____

_____

_____

What could you do to show those parts more?

_____

_____

The Gender Identity Workbook for Kids

How might this feel for you?

_____

Is there any part of what you feel, know, or like on the inside that you're not sure you can show on the outside—at least not yet?

_____

_____

_____

_____

What can you do to help yourself feel ok even when you don't feel like you can share who you are?

_____

_____

_____

The Three "Tents"
ConsisTENT, PersisTENT, InsisTENT

For You to Know

It can be difficult to understand and assert your gender identity if it feels different from what everyone else says or believes it is.

There are many ways people experience gender, so maybe you're not sure what your experience means. Are you a girl? Are you a boy? Are you neither or both or something else? Are you transgender? So many questions! Lots of people need help understanding their gender, especially children who feel their gender differently than people expect. It can be even harder when you don't feel that your gender fits neatly into a boy or girl box.

Transgender children have a few things in common that make them different from kids who are gender-expansive. Gender-expansive kids mostly feel like their gender is the same as their assigned sex (labeled a boy and feel like a boy, or told they were a girl and feel like a girl), but they feel best expressing their gender in ways people don't expect and sometimes aren't used to. This means that gender-expansive kids need more freedom and acceptance regarding their gender expression, not their gender identity. In contrast, transgender children feel, express, and/or know themselves in a gender that is different than their assigned sex. This means that transgender children often need more freedom and acceptance regarding their gender expression *and* their gender identity.

So how do we know if someone is transgender? Transgender kids usually experience their gender—knowing themselves as boys, girls, neither, both, or something else— as different from their assigned sex in ways that are *consistent*, *persistent*, and *insistent*. Those are some big words! Let's look at what they mean.

Consistent means continuing to happen in the same way over time.

A transgender child can feel like a girl, a boy, neither, both, or something else, and will share this with their words or through gender expressions such as clothes, hairstyles, toys, and activities. This feeling of being another gender stays about the same over months and years, even when a person's asserted gender is naturally fluid (a mix of girl and boy).

Persistent means continuing to happen over a long period of time—not stopping or going away.

A transgender child does not stop feeling like another gender. A transgender child who feels like another gender at age seven will likely continue to feel like that gender in high school and into adulthood. Keep in mind that it is natural for a transgender child to feel discomfort or to be hesitant about showing their true gender experience to others, especially if they don't feel supported by the people around them.

Insistent means demanding that something happen or that someone do something, making oneself difficult to ignore.

Some transgender children are clear and firm about knowing their gender at a young age. These children declare their gender—"I am not the gender you think I am!"—and they won't rest until people get it. That's an example of being insistent. But many transgender children struggle with letting people know about their gender, because they don't have the right words yet or they are unsure if people will accept them. Since kids are still growing and learning, some gender-expansive children just don't have their true gender in clear view yet. These kids benefit from more time to keep exploring. Other transgender kids just aren't the demanding type, so their journey may be quieter or slower. As you can see, not every transgender child will be insistent, or at least not insistent in the same way; but that doesn't mean they don't or can't know their own gender.

Understanding your gender and figuring out how it works can take time. I hope the ideas above help you to better understand the way you feel. It will be important to stay in touch with your gender as you grow. Sometimes experiences of gender can change—feelings can get stronger, shift, or fade. Perhaps you think you might be transgender and this feeling grows even stronger with time, making it more important that your true gender is expressed and affirmed by others. Perhaps you feel gender-expansive and later discover that you're transgender. If you feel lost, just try and accept where you are today and take each experience as it comes.

For You to Do

Consistent:

How long have you known yourself to be a gender that is different from your assigned sex?

_____

_____

How has feeling or expressing yourself like that gender stayed the same over time?

_____

_____

How has feeling or expressing yourself like that gender changed over time?

_____

_____

Persistent:

What gender do you know yourself to be now?

_____

_____

Have you ever felt something other than that gender? If so, what was that like?

_____

_____

_____

What gender do you think you will be five years from now? When you are an adult?

_____

_____

Insistent:

Who have you told about your gender?

_____

_____

How did you let them know about your gender?

_____

_____

_____

If you haven't told anyone, share what makes you feel like not telling.

_____

_____

_____

My Space in the Spectrum

For You to Know

Knowing yourself is the key to being yourself.

At this point in the book, we have learned a lot about gender, and now we know there is room for EVERYONE. In this activity, you get the chance to map out your own gender.

As helpful reminders, here's what we have learned about the parts of gender so far:

- **Assigned sex** is a label of boy or girl based on a quick look between a baby's legs. This is what your birth certificate says—Male or Female.

- **Gender expression** is the way people show their gender through hairstyles, clothes, activities, and interests. People often describe these as feminine (what people think girls like) or masculine (what people think boys like). Gender expression can also be more neutral or involve a mix of feminine and masculine qualities.

- **Gender identity** is your knowledge of yourself as a boy, a girl, neither, both, or something else.

For You to Do

There are so many places along the Gender Spectrum—find the space that fits you best!

1. **Assigned Sex:** What your birth certificate says:

   _____

   Male   Female

2. **Gender Expression:** Mark a spot on each line that describes you best. You can have a little or a lot of both.

   _____

   Gender-neutral   Masculine
   (Things anyone can wear or do)   (Things you see more boys wear or do)

   _____

   Gender-neutral   Feminine
   (Things anyone can wear or do)   (Things you see more girls wear or do)

The Gender Identity Workbook for Kids

3. **Gender Identity:** You can have a little or a lot of both. Mark a spot on each line that describes you best. If you prefer, use the space below these two lines to design your own way of showing your gender.

Gender-neutral   Boy

Gender-neutral   Girl

More to Do

Sex:

1. When you were born, did the doctors declare you were a boy or a girl?

    _____

2. What do you think the doctors got right about your assigned sex? What do you think they got wrong?

    _____

    _____

Gender Expression:

1. How do you like to wear your hair?

    _____

2. What kind of clothes do you like the best?

    _____

3. What are your favorite things to do?

    _____

4. Do you prefer things that girls usually like or things that boys usually like?

    _____

5. How would you like to express your gender differently, if it felt safe to do so?

    _____

6. Share a time you felt misunderstood or judged because of the way you expressed your gender. What, if anything, would you say now to the person who misunderstood or judged you?

_____

_____

Gender Identity:

1. How do you describe your gender? (Remember, you are the expert here!)

_____

_____

2. If you have a gender that is different than the label of boy or girl given to you when you were born, how do you feel about this difference?

_____

_____

3. If your gender identity is outside of the binary—outside of boy or girl—how does that feel for you?

_____

_____

4. Write down the names of two people who understand you and your gender identity.

_____

_____

My Birth Certificate

For You to Know

Birth certificates record your birth and are used to show people who you are. It feels best when this document reflects the true you.

A birth certificate is a paper that records a person's birth and includes, among many things, a person's name and gender. Sometimes the information placed on the birth certificate doesn't fit as a person grows. People may need to change the name given to them at birth or correct the gender marker that was recorded on the birth certificate.

Getting things right on this official document takes time, and it will require an adult's help. But in this activity, you have a chance to create a birth certificate that is just right for you.

For You to Do

Fill in the birth certificate on the next page with all the information that is right for you!

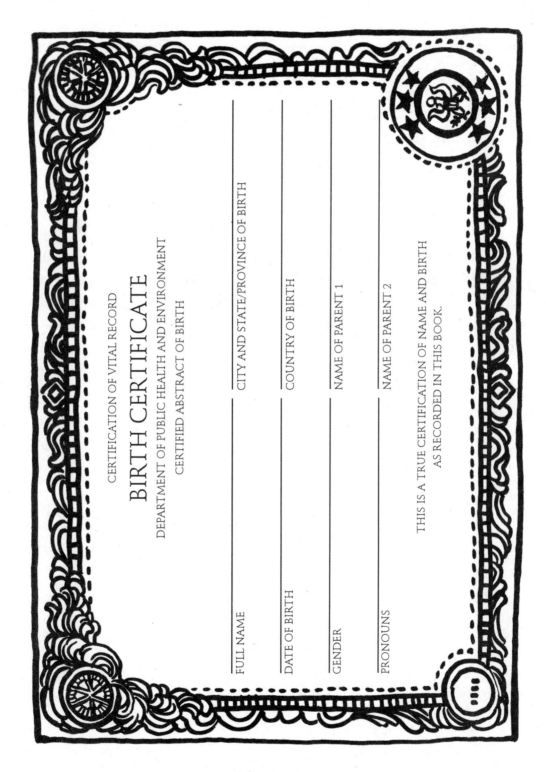

CERTIFICATION OF VITAL RECORD

BIRTH CERTIFICATE

DEPARTMENT OF PUBLIC HEALTH AND ENVIRONMENT

CERTIFIED ABSTRACT OF BIRTH

FULL NAME

CITY AND STATE/PROVINCE OF BIRTH

DATE OF BIRTH

COUNTRY OF BIRTH

GENDER

NAME OF PARENT 1

PRONOUNS

NAME OF PARENT 2

THIS IS A TRUE CERTIFICATION OF NAME AND BIRTH
AS RECORDED IN THIS BOOK.

Self-Portrait

For You to Know

You are amazing. You are beautiful. It's time to show it!

We've talked about how to see and love yourself in ways that create comfort and pride, no matter what your gender is. Here's a chance to create a self-portrait that reflects who you are when you feel most comfortable and proud, or what you would look like when you imagine yourself feeling comfortable and proud. On your mark, get set, draw!

For You to Do

Draw your most comfortable and proud self here—with the hair and clothes you like, in the place you like best, completely comfortable and happy.

More to Do

Describe your self-portrait.

_____

_____

_____

What feelings do you have when you see yourself in this portrait?

_____

_____

_____

Compared to a current photograph of you, what is different about you in this portrait? What is the same?

_____

_____

_____

Share this picture with someone who understands the true you so they can see YOU!

Section 3

Being Me

The final section of this book explores ideas and options for changes that can help gender-diverse kids like you live happy and healthy lives. If you feel the need to make changes so you can have your gender identity affirmed, many parts of a social transition are explored here. If you need help feeling safe and comfortable in your body, you will find information about how doctors assist gender-diverse kids.

What Is a Social Transition?

For You to Know

A social transition involves letting other people know and see your asserted gender—your true gender. This often includes changes in clothing, hairstyle, name, and pronouns.

When living in an ill-fitting gender feels stressful or sad, it can be helpful to think about making changes that relieve that stress and make you happier. When people make changes that help them be seen and accepted in the gender they know themselves to be, it *affirms* that identity. We can call that gender an asserted or *affirmed gender*. When people make changes to live in and express their affirmed gender, this is called a *social transition*. During a social transition, people make changes to things like their clothes, hairstyle, name, and pronouns so they better fit how the person feels. This might mean going by a different name, wearing different clothes, or changing the way they wear their hair. These changes make most transgender kids feel happier and more comfortable, but if they don't turn out to feel right, all these changes can be undone.

For You to Do

If you think a social transition might be right for you, what kind of changes—if any—would you like to make to your…

Clothes? _____

_____

Hair? _____

_____

Name? _____

_____

Pronouns? _____

_____

What feels important or necessary about the possibility of a social transition for you?

_____

_____

_____

_____

What feels uncomfortable about the idea of a social transition?

_____

_____

_____

_____

If you are considering or going through a social transition, what are you excited about the most?

_____

_____

_____

What scares you the most?

_____

_____

_____

More to Do

You might have a lot of questions about social transitions—what they are and how they work. Read on to explore more about whether a social transition is right for you.

The Gender Identity Workbook for Kids

Is Social Transition Right for Me?

> ## *For You to Know*
>
> A social transition often helps transgender people feel happier and more comfortable. Knowing if or when it's right for you involves some thinking and planning.

How do you know if a social transition is right for you?

Consistent, Persistent, Insistent: If the gender identity you're asserting feels about the same over time, and it consistently feels like something needs to be different, it's important to take this seriously. Remember, nobody can know your gender better than you.

Comfort/Distress: If you feel like your gender identity matches up with your assigned sex—labeled a boy and feel like a boy, labeled a girl and feel like a girl—there is probably no need to make changes. If you feel uncomfortable, sad, stressed, or unsafe with the gender placed on you by your assigned sex—labeled a boy or girl and feel like a different gender—it is time to consider changes that can help you feel more comfortable, happy, calm, and safe.

Adult Support: You need to have caregivers who understand your need to live in your own gender even when that gender is different than they expected. This means that your parents will need to learn about gender and to know as much as possible about your gender. This book can be super helpful for this part! It's really important to have this support, so if you don't have it yet, keep working to let the adults in your life know how important and real this is for you.

Safety: Do you have lots of worries or feel unsafe? Does it feel calmer or safer when you imagine getting to be your truest self? In a social transition, we want the changes to bring more happiness, safety, and comfort for the person as they get closer to living freely in their true gender. Considering big changes like a social transition can feel worrisome at first, but if it's right for someone and they have good supports, it should feel safer and happier as things move along. If things start to feel worse, people can always take a break, slow things down, or undo the changes. A social transition might not feel easy or risk-free, but it's important that the transition feels safe and right.

No child can go through a social transition alone. If what you've read here makes you feel like a social transition is right for you, it's important to share those thoughts and feelings with adults who can help you. Even if you're still not sure about social transition or whether it's something you want, it can help to talk to someone you're comfortable with about your thoughts and feelings. Together, you can get more information, think about various options, get support, and make any necessary plans. And remember, just reading this book is a wonderful step in finding out what is right for you.

For You to Do

Does your gender feel about the same over the most recent months or years?

Yes   Mostly   Sometimes   No

Has this gender stayed true for you, without going away?

Yes   Mostly   Sometimes   No

When you think about your gender, does it feel like you need some things to change? For example, would you like your clothes, hair, name, or pronouns to be different?

Yes   Mostly   Sometimes   No

Would you like people to know that you are a different gender than they used to think?

Yes   Mostly   Sometimes   No

Does living with your current gender (based on your assigned sex) make you feel uncomfortable, sad, stressed, or unsafe sometimes?

Yes   Mostly   Sometimes   No

Do the adults in your life, especially your parents or the people raising you, understand your asserted gender and support you in making changes?

Yes   Mostly   Sometimes   No

Do you feel happier, safer, or more comfortable when you think about making changes to live in your asserted gender?

Yes   Mostly   Sometimes   No

My Dream Room

For You to Know

Having spaces that showcase your style can help you feel happy and proud to be YOU.

Your bedroom is a great space to display who you are and what you like. You can express yourself through the color of your walls, the things you have around your room, and the bedding you choose. Sometimes kids' rooms don't fit them very well because their parents created the room before they really knew the unique qualities of their child. But as kids grow, rooms can change to reflect the growing person. These changes can be as small as adding a special stuffed animal and a cool poster or as big as repainting the walls and changing the furniture. You can work with your parents to make these changes and create a space that fits you. First, take some time to think about what your dream room would look like.

For You to Do

How does it feel to live in the room you have now?

_____

_____

_____

_____

What do you like about your room as it is now?

_____

_____

_____

What do you not like about your room as it is now?

_____

_____

_____

More to Do

Use the picture below to draw and color your dream room.

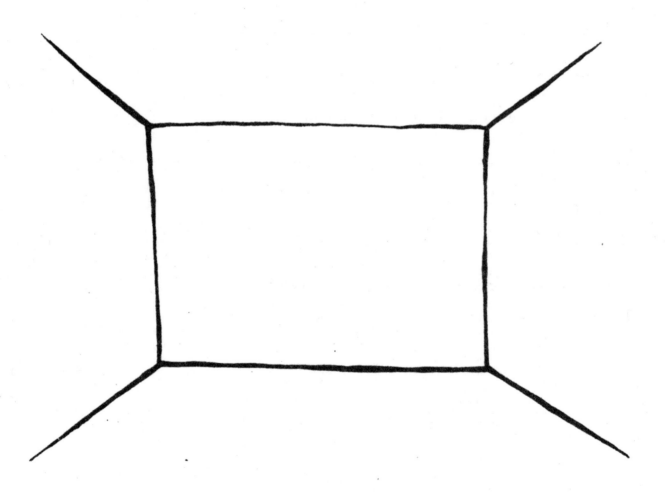

The Gender Identity Workbook for Kids

What are your favorite things about this dream room?

_____

_____

_____

How do you think it would feel to live in this dream room?

_____

_____

What is one small thing you can do to change your room now that will help it feel more like your dream room?

_____

_____

What are some bigger things you can do, perhaps with your parents' or siblings' help, in the future?

_____

_____

Parents Are VIPs—
Very Important People

For You to Know

Parents have a very important job in taking care of you. And you depend on your parents to do this job well. This makes parents very important people!

Many of the needs children have can only be met with the help or permission of their parents. This goes double for kids who are gender-expansive or transgender. Gender-diverse children like yourself have special needs that make it even more important that parents are informed, dependable, and loving.

Being yourself and getting your needs met can be difficult even when parents accept who you are. But with time and work, kids with affirming parents are usually quite happy and healthy. To push things along, keep talking with your parents and share this book with them. Things may move more slowly if your parents don't yet have the information they need about gender (there is help for them in this book, too!). And it can get complicated if you live apart from your parents or lack trust with them, or if one of your parents struggles with their health. All these things can make it hard for your parents to really be there for you. But even if it's slow or hard, keep going—you, your gender, and your needs are important!

The most painful of all parent situations is when a child shows and shares their true self to a parent who then rejects them or their gender. Some parents will yell or call names; others may refuse to acknowledge or listen. If you have parents who reject you or your gender, this can leave you feeling alone and scared. You probably feel

The Gender Identity Workbook for Kids

bad about being different and aren't sure what else to do since the people closest to you do not understand or accept you. This hurts, and I am so sorry that you have to carry this struggle.

First, I want you to know that this is not your fault. You are not wrong or bad or broken. Your parents have a wonderful child in you, and they need to do the work to take good care of you. Many parents get confused, worried, or sad when they don't fully understand what's going on. Some parents do not or will not get the information and support they need. We can hope they will eventually do better, that they will come to value and respect you, your thoughts, your feelings, and your needs related to your gender. But whether they do better or not is mostly out of your control. Whatever happens with your parents, you deserve support here and now.

So the second thing I want you to work on is to find an adult who you can trust to help you. This can be a relative, a family friend, a school teacher or counselor, a therapist, a doctor, or someone else like that. (You'll learn more about these people in Activity 28.) Tell this adult what's going on and let them know that you need their help because you don't feel supported by your parents. If you are being hurt by your parents—with mean words, physical violence, or sexual abuse—it is very important that you tell another adult. They can help you and they may be able to help work with your parents. The most important thing here is that you find someone who is safe and trustworthy and who affirms you as the beautiful, healthy, important child you are.

Activity 24 Parents Are VIPs—Very Important People

For You to Do

Mark the spot along this line that best describes how you see your parents' support or rejection of your asserted gender.

_____

Completely rejecting
(Do not accept you at all)

Completely supportive
(Accept you all the way)

How do your parents show their love and support for you and your gender?

_____

_____

_____

If you feel your parents are not accepting you or your gender, in what ways do you feel this rejection?

_____

_____

_____

What would you like your parents to do differently?

_____

_____

_____

If your parents are not helpful, write down two adults you can trust to help you.

_____

_____

Make a plan to talk with them so you get the help you need.

_____

_____

Siblings

For You to Know

Siblings can bring each other so much fun, help, love, and kindness. They can be annoying and frustrating too! Hopefully, you and your siblings can work together to get along and be supportive to each other.

Everyone in a family is worthy of love and support. Sometimes the siblings of a transgender or gender-expansive child can feel left out, less important, or under pressure when the family's energy is focused on that child's gender. And sometimes it's easy to get lost in the not-so-great parts of having a sibling, like their annoying behavior and the fights you have. Let's take this moment to remember that siblings can be wonderful friends, awesome helpers, and very loyal protectors who also need love and support.

For You to Do

Complete these sentences about each of your siblings. Share your answers with them.

My favorite things about having you as a sibling are... _____

_____

I am so thankful that you are my sibling because... _____

_____

My favorite things to do with you are... _____

_____

You have helped me through this gender journey by... _____

_____

One thing that could help us be even better siblings to each other is... _____

_____

_____

Now have your siblings complete the sentences about you!

My favorite things about having you as a sibling are… _____

_____

I am so thankful that you are my sibling because… _____

_____

My favorite things to do with you are… _____

_____

You have helped me through this gender journey by… _____

_____

One thing that could help us be even better siblings to each other is… _____

_____

Sharing Your Gender Activity 26

> ## *For You to Know*
>
> It's important that people know you well so they can love you well.

As you begin to understand yourself better, you will find that you need to talk with other people about your gender. Since it is a family's job to love and take care of the children, this sharing usually starts with the adults in your family. But it can start with anyone you feel safe with. Sharing about your gender can make you feel both relieved and nervous. The excited part of you may want to get it all done in one big swoop and the nervous part of you may want to run off and hide. This can feel overwhelming, so let's look at the why, what, who, how, and when of it all.

Why share with people?

1. We all need help and the people you share with can help YOU.

2. This is how you get to be YOU, the free and happy YOU.

3. Some adults may believe they know your gender, so when they have it wrong, you need to let them know the true YOU.

4. YOU are an awesome kid and YOU have nothing to hide!

Notice something here? Sharing your true and beautiful self is always about YOU. This is your story, your life, your gender, your feelings.

What should you share?

Everyone's sharing is unique, because every person and every story is unique. To start, just focus on what you want the person you're telling to know the most and the rest will come in time. You can start by telling them you want to share important information about yourself because you need their love and support. You can tell them that your gender is different than they might expect, or you can use the term "transgender" to help them understand how you feel. Feel free to use any of the activities in this book, if it helps!

Who should you share with?

It's best to share first with people who you know love and accept you no matter what. If it's not one of your parents, find a close adult (teacher, family friend, therapist) who has shown you that they have this unconditional love and support for you. Telling people you feel safe with gives you good helpers for your journey. Unfortunately, some kids have a hard time finding anyone who feels safe enough to tell, and they may have to wait until they can find a trustworthy person. Most often parents, siblings, or close friends are the first to know, followed by extended family (like cousins or grandparents), family friends, and other friends. If you share with a parent and they don't want anyone else to know, keep talking with them about how important it feels for other people to know and affirm your true self. If they don't change their minds soon, you may be forced to wait a while. Don't give up, especially on yourself. You are a wonderful kid and with some support and time, you can live more freely. Unfortunately, in some cases this means a kid has to wait until they are an adult or out of their family's house.

How should you share?

It's best if you can talk face-to-face with the adults closest to you. But if you don't feel quite ready for that, writing a letter can be a great way to share. A letter can help you feel ready for a talk, or you can read the letter to the adult as a way to start a talk. Telling extended family and adult friends is usually a job for parents or the people raising you, unless you want to be the one to share. You can work with these adults to figure out what's best for you.

When should you share?

Since you depend on adults, it's best to tell them as soon as you feel ready, so they can help you get the support you need. You might have already told a trusted adult, and that might be how you came to have this book. (I'm so glad!) Or you might not be able to find safe people to tell right away, and this may mean you have to wait to share until you find someone who will provide you with the love and support you deserve. Once your parents know, you can work together with them to figure out when to tell the other people in your life. You are still a kid, so just know that you do not have to figure this out on your own.

For You to Do

1. Make a list of people you would like to know more about you and your gender.

    _____ _____

    _____ _____

    _____ _____

2. Write some thoughts about what you want to share with these people. This will help you feel more prepared, or help your family know what to share.

    _____

    _____

    _____

    _____

3. What feels like the best way to share with these people? A few options: talking face-to-face, calling on the phone, writing a letter.

    _____

    _____

4. Make a list of people you do not want to know more about you and your gender. Do your best to describe why you aren't ready or do not want them to know.

_____

_____

_____

_____

_____

5. List at least two people you trust to help you talk to other people.

_____

_____

More to Do

1. It's important to keep track of your feelings as you share your experiences related to gender. Circle the feelings you are having about sharing with people in your life.

Excited	Worried	Relieved	Curious
Nervous	Frustrated	Eager	Mad
Happy	Sad	Embarrassed	Scared

2. What do you like about having people know more about you and your gender?

_____

_____

3. Share any worries you have about people knowing more about you and your gender.

_____

_____

_____

The Gender Identity Workbook for Kids

Helpers Are for Helping Activity 27

For You to Know

Helpers are workers who support people when they are in need. Everyone—kids and adults alike—needs a helper sometimes. The best part of having helpers? They *help*!

There are all kinds of adults—therapists, doctors, school staff, lawyers—who are experts in helping others get what they need. Many adults make good helpers by the way they listen to you, care about what's happening for you, help you get what you need, and respect you and your gender, all while watching out for your well-being and safety. Those are some of the things that make people good helpers. Keep in mind that just because someone is an adult does not automatically make them right or safe. In fact, sometimes an adult doesn't understand gender and gender-diverse people well, and those adults can be harmful instead of helpful. If you ever feel hurt, rejected, scared, ignored, or shamed by an adult who is supposed to help, you do not have to keep sharing with that person. And if you have another adult you trust, let them know how you feel about the unhelpful adult so they can find you a safer helper.

What do these helpers do for people?

Therapists help people understand feelings, tend to problems, and cope with difficult situations.

Medical providers—like doctors and nurse practitioners—help people understand medical issues and take care of their bodies so they can be healthy.

School staff—like teachers, principals, and counselors—help create safe schools that support every student as they learn and grow.

Lawyers help people understand and work within the rules or laws that guide us and the places we go, like schools and hospitals. Sometimes lawyers work to change rules that aren't fair!

How can these helpers help you, as someone who is gender-expansive or transgender?

Therapists:

- Help you learn more about your gender and how you live with your gender.

- Help you deal with hard things like feeling scared or sad, being bullied, or not liking yourself or your body.

- Help you feel understood, accepted, and affirmed.

- Help your family understand, accept, and affirm you.

Doctors:

- Help you be safe and healthy, especially if you feel uncomfortable in your body.

- Help you and your parents learn about medical options available to you as you grow.

- They are especially important at *puberty*—when your kid body starts changing into an adult body. (More on this in Activity 34.)

School staff:

- Help you be yourself at school—go to school as a boy, a girl, neither, both, or something else.

- Help you feel safe and supported in your gender at school.

- Help address any problems you might experience at school.

Lawyers:

- Help your parents understand your legal rights, including your rights in school, changing your name or gender markers, and getting medical care.

- Help protect your legal rights in case people try to do things that are unfair or hurtful.

For You to Do

Which helpers, from the list above, would you like to have help you?

_____

_____

_____

What would you like them to help you with? See the lists above for ideas or add your own.

_____

_____

_____

Being You at School

For You to Know

Being safe and comfortable at school is really important. Having your gender identity and expression recognized and affirmed at school helps you feel ready to learn and grow.

Students spend about 1,000 hours in school each year. That's a lot of time in one place, and so it's really important that your school feels like a safe place where you can grow and learn. School is about much more than math, science, writing, and history. School is the place where you develop into yourself as a person and learn how to be in all kinds of different relationships. Teachers show us not only how to read and write, but also how to be a respectful person and how to relate to classmates and adults. All kids are practicing how to be good friends by listening to each other, sharing with each other, and treating each other with respect. When school staff and classmates are kind and fair, you are ready to do your best each day.

But what if you feel out of place at school because people have your gender wrong? Or what if your peers tease or bully you about your gender or gender expressions? And what if you're thinking about sharing your asserted gender or making changes to your gender expression and you're nervous about how people at school will react? This can make school an unpleasant or even unsafe place. Schools should be safe, welcoming places for all kids, and if you are struggling at school, you, your parents, and the school staff can work to make things better.

First, let's think about how you want to go to school. Going to school as your boy, girl, gender-expansive, or non-binary self can help you feel safe, valued, and able to learn. Things like changing your name or pronouns, getting support, having friends, and finding the right bathroom can feel challenging. If you're making a social transition, that calls for change, and change can be hard. Some students choose to share their newly asserted or affirmed gender and stay at their school, while other students choose to change their schools and start anew in their affirmed gender. If you change schools, you will want to think about whether to keep your assigned sex private or allow others to know that you are transgender. Keep in mind that your feelings and approach to this question may change as you get older.

If you stay in your school for your social transition, there are several things to think about with your parents or the people raising you. Sometimes kids have already told a teacher or counselor; other times no adult at school knows about a child being transgender or needing to transition. Either way, it's best to put together a team of people to plan a successful transition. This almost always involves the principal, but may also include a trusted teacher, a counselor or social worker, or a nurse. Your parents or the people raising you can call a meeting with this team to discuss your needs and how the school can best meet those needs. Here are some areas to think about when changing things at school:

Changes to name or pronouns: You or your parents can let the school know what name and pronouns you will be using. All school staff need to use this name and your pronouns once your transition is in place. If your old name or pronouns are used (especially more than once by the same person), you can correct the person as it happens, talk with them later to remind them, or have one of your support people at school (check the next section) help you make sure that people use the correct name and pronouns.

Support: You will have a team of trusted helpers in school so you know who to turn to if you have any problems or needs. These folks will be available to you at any time, but it is especially important that you talk with them if you don't know how to handle a situation or you are having a problem (being teased, kids asking unwanted questions, feeling uncomfortable in the bathroom).

Bathrooms: Finding the right bathroom can be tricky. If the school has gender-neutral or all-gender bathrooms, you are certainly free to use those. Many kids simply start using the bathroom of their asserted or affirmed gender once transition is in place. Many schools can make a staff or nurse's office bathroom available to transgender students. Keep in mind that using an entirely separate bathroom only works if you *choose* it—no one should be forced to use separate bathrooms just because they are transgender.

Records: Your name should be changed, even if it's not legally changed yet, in as many places as possible to make for a safe and positive transition. School staff will need to check lists in the cafeteria, library, teacher's files, and so on. By law, your records should remain private and protected. This means that staff cannot share information about you or your gender with other students or families.

For You to Do

Would you like to go to school as your boy, girl, gender-expansive, or non-binary self (different from the gender your school now thinks of you)?

Yes   No

If no, maybe you simply don't need changes, or don't need changes now. You can always take your time and only move ahead with changes when it feels right for you. You can skip the next steps in this activity or use them to think about options for your future.

If yes, what would you like to be different about how you go to school?

_____

_____

_____

What name and pronouns do you want to use at school? _____

Would you rather stay in your school or change schools? _____

If you want to change schools, what kind of school do you think is best?

_____

_____

Would you want people to know you are transgender, or would you rather keep that information private?

_____

_____

If you want to stay in your present school:

Who do you want on the team that helps plan and support your transition?

_____

_____

_____

Which bathroom do you want to use once your transition is in place?

_____

_____

Name anyone, child or adult, you are worried might be unkind or unfair to you. Who or what might help you deal with them?

_____

_____

_____

I Don't Have a Secret, Activity 29
I Have Privacy

For You to Know

Keeping things private can help people, keeping things secret can hurt people.

We all have things about us, like thoughts and feelings, that other people can't easily see just by looking at us. It's natural to keep some of these things just for you or the people closest to you to know. This is called keeping things *private*. Most of the time, you get to choose if people know personal things about you. You get to choose what and when to share personal things with another person. You also have the right to have the people who know personal things about you protect your privacy by not telling anyone else, unless you tell them it's okay to share with someone. (There's just one exception: If the personal, private thing is something that could hurt you, then people may need to share it to help keep you safe.)

At times, keeping information about yourself private can help you feel more comfortable and safe. Sometimes people feel scared to share parts of themselves because they think they're bad or they worry people will treat them unkindly. When you want to share more about yourself but you feel you have to hide parts of yourself because you are afraid of being hurt or rejected, this isn't exactly privacy—it's called keeping things *secret*. People who keep things secret often don't feel like they have a choice—they believe that if they share the secret something bad will happen. Keeping something a secret often makes people feel alone, worried, and ashamed.

You might have some things that are private—"inside stuff" you share with just the people you trust because you feel better that way. There might also be things you're keeping secret. You might be leaving out some "inside stuff" that's really important to you and important to share because you're afraid people just won't understand. It's possible to turn things that feel like secrets into things that are honored as private. To do this, you will need to find the right person to share them with. If someone shows you love and kindness when you share such personal things with them, this can help you feel happier and calmer. Sharing also helps you build a team of people who know you and can help you.

Here are some examples of how kids keep some personal things private because it feels good, as compared to how sometimes kids hold on to secrets because they are afraid they can't share and they end up feeling stressed and uncomfortable. I want you to see the difference so you don't have to hold on to secrets that hurt you.

Private:

- You share lots of your feelings about gender with your parents, who love you and help you. You don't share these feelings with your grandpa, who yells at you or teases you. Privacy isn't an all-or-nothing thing—you can share more with the people you trust.

- A kid at school asks you what your body looks like under your clothes. Since this isn't anyone's business but your own, you tell them, "Bodies are private and I don't talk about that."

- Someone asks why you "act like a boy/girl" and you reply, "I am just being me. I do what makes me happy." You get to choose when you share details about your gender or gender expressions.

Secret:

- You never say that you feel different about your gender, because you worry that your parents and friends will reject you and won't understand.

- You pretend to be a boy or girl when you really feel like another gender, because you are afraid people will tell you that you are bad or wrong.

- A parent yells, "Boys don't wear dresses," and sends you to your room. So even though you love how dresses feel on you, you don't let anyone see you in a dress again.

For You to Do

Write down any secrets—things that you feel you have to hide—about your gender. If you aren't ready to share here, just think about them in your mind as you read the questions below.

_____

_____

_____

What are you afraid will happen if you share these secrets with people?

_____

_____

_____

What would make you feel safe enough to share?

_____

_____

_____

Write down two people you would like to share these secret thoughts or feelings with.

_____

_____

How to Handle Questions

For You to Know

Practicing how you want to respond to possible questions can help you feel prepared when or if people ask you about your gender.

Human beings are naturally curious—people love to figure things out. When people can't figure out someone's gender or they feel like that person's gender is different than they expected, they can be especially full of questions. Some questions are because people are trying to understand, so they can do a better job in talking to you and treating you with respect. Some other questions arise from curiosity—and even if people don't mean to hurt you, the questions they ask can be uncomfortable or inappropriate. Some of these questions—the hardest ones of all to deal with—are from people who are purposely trying to disrespect, tease, or bully you. To help you feel more prepared to deal with all these kinds of questions, we will go over some common ones, as well as a few answers that you can mix and match as you like.

Question: What are you *really*, a boy or a girl?

- Gender is a person's own knowledge of themself as a boy, a girl, neither, both, or something else.

- I am a girl/boy/neither/both/something else (if you want to share).

- All genders are real.

Question: Did you used to be a boy/girl?

- I have always been a girl/boy/neither/both/something else (if you want to share). That's it.

- People used to think I was a boy/girl, but I am a girl/boy/neither/both/ something else.

Question: Are you transgender?

- I don't know what you are talking about.

- That's private and I don't feel like talking about that with you.

- Yes. And proud!

- No. (Because you don't have to tell anyone you don't want to tell.)

Question: What kind of body/body parts do you have? Are you going to change your body?

- Bodies are private, so I'm not talking about that.

- I don't ask about your body, so please don't ask about mine.

Question: You can't be both a girl and a boy, so which one are you really?

- People can be both a boy and a girl. I know because I am.

- It's called being non-binary/gender-fluid, and it is real.

- Many people don't know it, but you can be both. Pretty cool, huh?

Question: Why do you want to be a boy/girl/neither/both/something else?

- I don't *want* to be a boy/girl/neither/both/something else. I *am* a boy/girl/neither/both/something else.

- This is how I feel happiest. I like being me.

Question: Why do you wear dresses and skirts?

- Because they are amazing!

- I wear clothes that make me feel comfortable and happy. Just like you do.

- Some people think boys shouldn't wear skirts. I think that's a silly rule.

Question: What does it mean to be transgender?

- Being transgender means that a person's gender is different from the sex assigned to them when they were born.

Question: How are things going for you?

- Things are awesome/good/okay/hard. (Share as much or as little detail as you wish.)

- Thanks for caring to ask about how things are going for me.

- They're okay. How about you?

For You to Do

Write down your favorite answers to any or all of these questions:

What are you *really*, a boy or a girl?

_____

_____

Did you used to be a boy/girl?

_____

_____

Are you transgender?

_____

_____

What kind of body/body parts do you have? Are you going to change your body?

_____

_____

You can't be both a girl and a boy, so which one are you really?

_____

_____

Why do you want to be a boy/girl/neither/both/something else?

_____

_____

Why do you wear dresses and skirts?

_____

_____

What does it mean to be transgender?

_____

_____

How are things going for you?

_____

_____

You can use any of these answers any time someone asks you one of these questions. Remember that you don't have to share anything you don't want to or answer questions that don't feel appropriate.

Activity 31 Gender and Religion

For You to Know

It's hard to know what's "right" when it comes to believing, or not believing, in gods and religions. There is one thing you should know: If anyone or anything rejects or shames any part of you in the name of religion, that's not right.

Religion is the worship of a god, gods, or other superhuman higher powers. For many people, religion is a way to find meaning in the world. They use its teachings to help guide their thoughts, feelings, and behaviors. Like gender, religion is a part of our world that has a lot of variety. This means lots of different people have lots of different beliefs. In many ways, the practice of religion brings great comfort to people, and a sense of unity. But sometimes religious views are used to shame and reject people. This is harmful and shouldn't happen, especially to children.

Many religions and places of worship proudly welcome all different kinds of people. The religion you or your family follows might be a great source of support for you, and if it is, that's wonderful. In certain religions and places of worship, people may misunderstand, reject, and speak against people they deem different or "sinful." Gender-expansive and transgender people are some of the people who are most often rejected and hurt in these ways.

I hope this never happens to you. But if it does, here are a few things I want to make sure you know:

1. If someone tells you "God doesn't make mistakes. You are a [sex assigned at birth], not a [asserted or affirmed gender]": It's true that "God doesn't make mistakes"—you were born to be just what you are, a gender-expansive person or a transgender person. You are a blessing to this world and should be treated as such.

2. With so many different religions and belief systems, no one can say that their way is the absolute right and only way. Everyone gets to choose their own religion and no one has the right to force their views, especially hurtful ones, on anyone else.

3. Religious leaders, like priests and preachers and rabbis, are human, just like you. And no human has the right to judge and reject you, no matter how important or powerful they are.

4. If you don't feel safe and loved in your place of worship, let your family know and ask them to find a place that understands how amazing you are. If your family insists on holding on to a religion that rejects you or stays in a hurtful place of worship, please know that there are people and places all over the world that love and value you for being you.

5. Even in religions and places of worship that don't understand or respect gender diversity, you might find wonderful people who know better and who will offer you love and support. Keep yourself as safe and comfortable as possible until you can find them. Talk to teachers or other adults who could help, or other kids who make you feel loved and supported.

For You to Do

Do you or your family practice a religion? If so, which one? _____

In what ways do you feel safe and supported within your religion or place of worship?

_____

_____

In what ways do you feel hurt or rejected within your religion or place of worship?

_____

_____

Sometimes people need to make changes when a religion or place of worship refuses to respect them. If you need a change like that, what feels like the right thing for you or your family to do now?

_____

_____

_____

More to Do

Many people find it helpful to talk directly with their god when they are hurting, or when they feel something powerful they don't know what to do about. If this feels right for you, write a letter here describing how you feel about being gender-expansive or transgender.

Dear _____,

_____

_____

_____

_____

_____

_____

_____

Sincerely,

_____

Peeing in Peace

For You to Know

Bathrooms should be safe spaces for everyone. People should be free to use the bathroom that fits their gender.

Everyone has to pee, right? Going to the bathroom is a basic human need, and having a public bathroom that feels safe to use should be a right for every person. Unfortunately, bathrooms can be very tricky spaces for transgender and gender-expansive people. In fact, some people avoid using public bathrooms because they don't have an option that feels right for them, and this can be bad for a person's health.

Because young children need help using the restroom, adults start off by taking them into whatever bathroom they already use—or a private family bathroom, if there is one. This back-and-forth use of the bathrooms—family, girls', or boys'—usually works well when kids are little. But when it's time to choose what bathroom you will use on your own, it can get tricky, especially if the bathroom that people expect you to use (the one that fits your assigned sex) doesn't feel right or comfortable for you.

Many gender-expansive or transgender people, especially when they are first figuring things out, feel most comfortable using bathrooms that provide the most privacy. Family restrooms or single-use bathrooms can feel safest because you can use them without running into other people. But since it can be hard to find these private bathrooms, you will eventually find yourself needing to choose between using a girls' bathroom and a boys' bathroom. Which door should you choose?

Magic Wand Experiment

Experiment

> ## *For You to Know*
>
> Gender-diverse people, especially transgender people, often feel a need for their bodies to be different than they were born with, or different from how their body changes as they grow older. Understanding how you need your body to look and feel is an important step in getting those needs met.

It's common for transgender people, and some gender-expansive people, to feel uneasy or even downright miserable with parts of their bodies. The feeling that parts don't feel or fit right, or that you are supposed to have parts that aren't there, arises from the mismatch between the gender you know and the body you have. This discomfort regarding bodies and gender can be long and hard. As you grow older, there will be opportunities to change some of these things. Many people eventually make these changes, and other people live with the body they have and are happy that way.

For You to Do

Imagine you have a magic wand that has the power to effortlessly and painlessly change your body. From head to toe, write or draw on the figure below to show the way you want your body to look. If you don't want to change anything, feel free to skip this step or draw the body you already have.

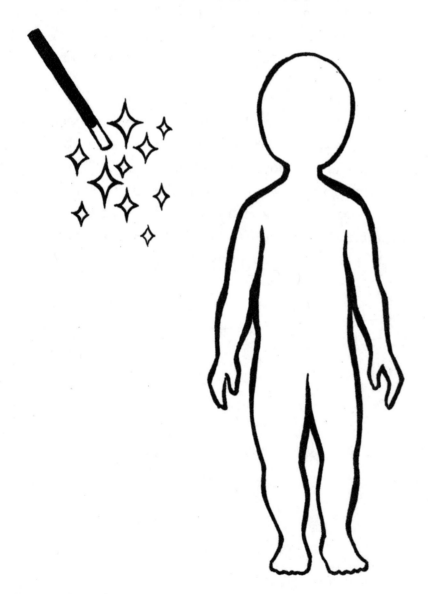

The Gender Identity Workbook for Kids

Magic Wand Experiment

More to Do

Describe the body you made for yourself.

_____

_____

What did you change from the body you have now?

_____

_____

What did you keep the same?

_____

_____

How does it feel to imagine having the body you wish for?

_____

_____

_____

What magic wand changes feel the most important to you?

_____

_____

_____

A Guide to Exploring Who You Are

131

Your Important and Changing Body

For You to Know

As your kid body grows into an adult body, medical providers—like doctors or nurse practitioners—have options that can help you feel more safe and comfortable in your body.

Many (but not all) transgender people feel discomfort about their bodies. For people who feel this discomfort, especially when these experiences are strong, this usually means they need help getting their body to feel right and safe for them. Doctors can help make this happen.

Most babies and children have bodies that look about the same except for their genitalia—the front parts of the body covered by a diaper or underwear. Then somewhere between the ages of eight and fourteen, a child's body begins to change into an adult's body through a process called *puberty*. Puberty, which unfolds over several years, happens when our brain sends out signals for our body to make hormones that direct our bodies to grow and change.

Some of these changes happen to all bodies, regardless of assigned sex:

Grow taller	Gain weight	Sweat more/body odor
Body changes shape	Skin gets oily/acne	New hair—underarms/pubic area
Muscles get stronger	Get more emotional	Bodies are able to make babies

There are also some differences in the way bodies change.

For people who are assigned a female sex at birth:

Grow breasts	Body gets rounder/ curvier	Period/menstruation starts

For people who are assigned a male sex at birth:

Penis grows	Testes get bigger	Hair grows on face
Penis can get erect/hard	Voice deepens	"Adam's apple" grows on front of neck

All these changes can be overwhelming for any kid, but they can be especially overwhelming for transgender kids. Some kids have felt uneasy about how their body connects to their gender for a long time before puberty, while other kids only start to feel this discomfort when puberty hits. Either way, when you know yourself to be a boy and you start to grow breasts, it can be scary and sad. Or when you know yourself to be a girl and your penis grows or your voice deepens, this can be scary and sad. If you loved having a kid body that felt neutral or fluid, the loss of this freedom can be scary and sad too. One thing I want you to understand as you read this book is that all bodies are important; no body is "wrong" or "bad." But if you're transgender and you have a strong need for parts of your developing body to be different than they are, it can be hard to feel good about your body. When these feelings get in the way of a child being happy and healthy, it's wise to understand options that can help. You can talk to your family about what you need and work with helpers like a doctor or therapist to see what might be available.

Once a person starts puberty, doctors can prescribe *puberty blockers*. These medications pause puberty so that a kid's body stops developing in ways that don't feel right. Stopping the unwanted changes can be incredibly relieving, and this treatment gives everyone time to work on what's best for the growing child. Puberty blockers are relatively safe and the effects are reversible. So if you find that you don't need your body to be different after all, you can stop the puberty blocker medication and everything will move along as it was before treatment, usually within a few months. If you find that you definitely need your body to develop differently, then you and your team of helpers can talk about *hormone therapy* as you get a little older.

Hormone therapy involves the use of hormones, prescribed and monitored by a doctor, to direct the body to develop in feminine or masculine ways. The feminizing form of hormone therapy leads to changes like breast growth, a softer body and face shape, and less hair on the body and face. The masculinizing form of hormone therapy leads to changes like a deeper voice and the growth of facial hair, and prevents or stops breast growth (but it will not take away any breast growth that has already occurred).

Deciding whether or not this sort of medical help is right for you is a super important decision that involves at least your parents or caregivers and a medical professional like a doctor. You may also need or want the aid of a therapist, who can help you and your family feel supported and informed as you make decisions. Having adults who know and respect your thoughts, feelings, and needs is key to making this right for you.

For You to Do

Write down any thoughts or questions you have about…

your body: _____

_____

puberty: _____

_____

options for medical help as you grow: _____

_____

Who would you most like to talk to about these things? Circle as many as you want.

Parent	The doctor you already have	A special doctor/ gender specialist
Therapist	Another trusted adult— write their name here:	Other: _____
	_____	

More to Do

Complete these sentences:

When I think about sharing these thoughts, feelings, and questions about my body with adults,

I feel excited about… _____

I feel worried about… _____

For You to Know

Growing up can be hard. Growing up feeling different can be even harder. We all need to have some help to keep us feeling safe, loved, and valued when times get hard.

Figuring out who you are can be overwhelming and challenging. Sometimes, figuring out how to be you out in the world can make things even harder. Most people still have a lot to learn about how gender really works, which means that people won't always understand you or your gender. When people don't understand, they can do and say things that hurt.

What can you do to take good care of yourself? We've already talked a lot about finding trusted and loving people to help you. Surrounding yourself with people who love, affirm, and celebrate you can be the most powerful tool you have. But you have another amazing tool that is always close by—YOU! There are things you can do to calm yourself that will help you bounce back from stuff that's hard so you can feel like you're safe, loved, and valued.

For You to Do

Circle any of these self-care tools that you use or would like to use. Add your own ideas in the spaces provided.

Listen to music	Spend time with a pet	Take a walk
Make art	Cry	Write in a journal
Take deep breaths	Read	Quiet time/pray or meditate
Play sports	Play a video game	Get something healthy to eat/drink

Write down your two favorite tools, and when and how you can use them.

Tool:	*When I can use this tool:*
1. *Listen to music*	1. *When I am sad at home*
2.	2.
3.	3.

The Gender Identity Workbook for Kids

Gender Is Just a Part of Me

For You to Know

Your gender is important, but it is only one part of the amazing YOU.

You have many talents, interests, feelings, and experiences that do not center around your gender. Sometimes we can lose track of that when gender takes up a lot of space in our thoughts. It's natural to think a lot about gender as you work to understand yourself better, but we all need to remember that we are so much more than our gender.

For You to Do

Here are some questions about other parts of your life—the things you like, the people you love, your experiences, and what you wish for. They'll help you see what a wonderful, awesome person you are!

1. The things I enjoy doing the most are… _____

   _____

2. I am a good friend when I… _____

   _____

3. I am a proud learner. The three things I enjoy most about school are…

   _____

   _____

   _____

4. My favorite foods are… _____.

   My least favorite foods are… _____.

5. The people I love most in the world are… _____

   _____

6. I would like to learn how to… _____

_____

7. When I grow up, I want to… _____

_____

8. The greatest thing that has ever happened to me is… _____

_____

9. If I had three wishes… _____

_____

More to Do

Sometimes it can be hard to quiet the pressures of your gender. If that is true for you, try asking your gender to take a rest. Go ahead, write a note to let your gender know you need some time to enjoy or deal with something else.

Dear Gender,

_____

_____

_____

_____

_____

_____

_____

Sincerely,

_____

Highs and Lows

For You to Know

Thinking and learning about your gender can be full of ups and downs. Tip: Enjoy the good stuff and get support for the hard stuff.

I hope this book has helped you and your family understand you and your gender better. I also hope that means you are getting more of what you need to feel happy and comfortable. While parts of this journey might have been difficult, I hope that most of it brought you joy and relief. As this book comes to a close, let's look back at the highs and lows of your journey so far.

For You to Do

HIGHS:

1. My favorite parts of this book were... _____

   _____

2. The three most important things I learned about myself are... _____

   _____

3. It was nice to work through this book with... _____.

   What I liked best about doing this with them was... _____

   _____

4. I am most excited about... _____

   _____

LOWS:

1. The most difficult parts of this book were... _____

   _____

2. I felt most sad when thinking about... _____

_____

3. I am worried about... _____

_____

4. I did not like it when... _____

_____

For your continued journey:

1. When I am having a hard time, it helps me to... _____

_____

2. I would feel even better if... _____

_____

3. I would like to know more about... _____

_____

4. What I want people to understand better is... _____

_____

Glossary

Agender: often used to describe someone who feels they do not identify with any gender at all.

Assigned sex: label of boy or girl based on a quick look between a newborn baby's legs. This is the label of male or female that goes on a baby's birth certificate.

Gender: a person's deep-down feeling that they are a boy, a girl, neither, both, or something else. A person's asserted or *affirmed gender* is the gender they know themself to be, not the one other people expect based on their assigned sex.

Gender binary: the belief that gender only comes in two forms—boy and girl. This leaves out people who have bodies that don't fit neatly into boy or girl, and all the people who have a gender beyond girl or boy.

Gender expression: the way a person "wears" or expresses their gender, including the way a person styles their hair, what clothes they wear, what they like to do, and how they act.

Gender-fluid: often used to describe someone whose gender moves between girl and boy or feels like a mix of both boy and girl.

Genderqueer: often used to describe someone who doesn't feel like either a girl or a boy.

Hormones: chemicals in a person's body that, in part, determine how a body changes during puberty.

Hormone therapy: a medical treatment that uses hormones, prescribed and monitored by a doctor, to direct the body to develop in typically feminine or masculine ways.

Intersex: describes someone whose body does not fit neatly into the expectations for either sex.

Non-binary: a person who is non-binary has a gender that is both boy and girl, neither boy nor girl, or something else not involving the two-option system of boy/girl.

Puberty: the process in which a child's body begins to change into an adult body.

Puberty blockers: medications that pause puberty so that a kid's body stops developing in ways that don't feel right.

Social transition: a process in which people make changes to live in their asserted or affirmed gender. A social transition often involves changes to things like clothes, hairstyle, name, and pronouns.

Transgender: a person who is transgender has an assigned sex and gender that are different. This happens when the label of boy or girl given to a person at birth does not fit who they know themself to be as a boy, a girl, neither, both, or something else.

Kelly Storck, LCSW, is a licensed clinical social worker with a private therapy practice in St. Louis, MO. Kelly's focus is in gender care and advocacy for transgender rights. Along with this work, Kelly presents workshops and trainings on issues relevant to gender diversity with intent to help support the greater health, well-being, and liberty of people of all genders.

Photo Credit to Nancy Stevens.

Foreword writer **Diane Ehrensaft, PhD**, is director of mental health, and a founding member of the UCSF Benioff Children's Hospital Child and Adolescent Gender Center Clinic. She is a developmental and clinical psychologist in the San Francisco Bay Area.

Illustrator **Noah Grigni** is an artist from Atlanta, GA, and is currently based in Boston, MA. His art focuses on themes of queer resilience, self-love, inward healing, navigating dysphoria, and finding strength in community. Through art and advocacy, he hopes to provide resources to trans kids. You can see his work at www.noahgrigni.com.

MORE BOOKS *from*
NEW HARBINGER PUBLICATIONS

Register your **new harbinger** titles for additional benefits!

When you register your **new harbinger** title— purchased in any format, from any source—you get access to benefits like the following:

- Downloadable accessories like printable worksheets and extra content

- Instructional videos and audio files

- Information about updates, corrections, and new editions

Not every title has accessories, but we're adding new material all the time.

Access free accessories in 3 easy steps:

1. Sign in at NewHarbinger.com (or **register** to create an account).

2. Click on **register a book**. Search for your title and click the **register** button when it appears.

3. Click on the **book cover or title** to go to its details page. Click on **accessories** to view and access files.

That's all there is to it!

If you need help, visit:

NewHarbinger.com/accessories

new harbinger
CELEBRATING
40 YEARS